THE WHAT KIND OF FOOD AM I? SERIES

•

*"You may never point at a menu
or at someone else's plate again."*
~ Chicago Tribune

"It makes dining...easy and enjoyable."
~ Toronto Sun

*"It's small, unobtrusive...and artfully designed -
the perfect holiday gift."*
~ Milwaukee Journal Sentinel

*"Providing a depth that general
phrasebooks lack."*
~ Midwest Book Review

Eating & Drinking in Spanish is
*"a dietary dictionary to help you decipher
'ropa vieja' as shredded beef, not old clothes!"*
~ Caribbean Travel & Life

D1117883

Also available in the
What Kind of Food Am I? Series

Eating and Drinking in Spanish:
Reading Menus in Spanish Speaking Countries
Capra Press, ISBN 0-88496-411-6

Soon to be available in the
What Kind of Food Am I? Series

Eating and Drinking in France:
Reading Menus in French

·

THE WHAT KIND OF FOOD AM I? SERIES

EATING & DRINKING IN ITALY

Reading Menus in Italian

Andy Herbach and Michael Dillon

CAPRA PRESS
SANTA BARBARA

*Thanks to Noel Young and David Dahl at Capra Press,
Marian Olson for the series title and her opinions
(and she has many of them), research assistants Mark
Berry and Dan Schmidt (they ate and drank a lot while
researching), Angelina Scharlau (our thorough and
helpful Italian editor) and travel writer Margo Classé
for all of her encouragement and help.*

•

Cover design and illustrations
by Michael Dillon.

LIBRARY OF CONGRESS
CATALOGING-IN-PUBLICATION DATA

Herbach, Andy.
   Eating & drinking in Italy : reading menus in Italian / Andy
Herbach & Michael Dillon.
      p. cm. -- (What kind of food am I? series)
   ISBN 0-88496-437-X (paper : alk. paper)
   1. Food--Dictionaries--Italian. 2. Cookery--Dictionaries--
Italian. 3. Italian language--Dictionaries--English. I. Dillon,
Michael. II. Title. III. Series.
TX350.H527 1999
641.3'0945'03--dc21   99-55570
                                                                    CIP

CAPRA PRESS
Post Office Box 2068
Santa Barbara, CA 93120

The *What Kind of Food Am I?* Series
Eating & Drinking in Italy
Introduction

Can you imagine a foreign traveler who speaks basic English understanding what prime rib is? Or a porterhouse? Veggie platter anyone? Buffalo wings? Sloppy joes?

Even people who speak passable Italian can have trouble reading a menu. You may know *ricotta* cheese, but not *malfatti di ricotta* which means "badly made," a reference to the handmade dumpling with *ricotta* cheese filling. You may be surprised to find *puttanesca* (which means *in the style of a prostitute*) on the menu. It is a sauce of tomatoes, capers, black olives and garlic.

Understanding the customs and food of a country helps travelers understand the people who live in the country.

If you love to travel as we do, you know the importance of a good guide. The same is true of dining. A good guide can make all the difference between a memorable evening and a dizzyingly bad one. This guide will help you find your way around a menu written in Italian. It gives you the freedom to enter places you might never have before and order a dinner without shouting, pointing and hand waving. Instead of fumbling with a bulky, conspicuous tourist guide (most of which usually includes a very incomplete listing of foods) in a restaurant, this book is a pocket-sized alphabetical listing of food and drink commonly found on menus in Italy.

Although, now that we think about it, a dinner without shouting and hand waving is not truly Italian.

Of course, traveling to a foreign country means something different to everyone. For every vacation there are different expectations, different needs, and every traveler has his or her own idea of what will make that vacation memorable. For us, the making of a memorable vacation begins and ends with food.

We spent the morning staring at the Sistine Chapel and the Vatican Museum, but what stands out in our minds is the wonderful lunch in the *trattoria* afterward. Although the waiter was less than helpful (in fact, not helpful at all), the creamy shrimp pasta dish was as heavenly as the Sistine Chapel. We spent a morning driving to see the Leaning Tower of Pisa, but the grilled lamb in Lerici made the day.

We know the panic of opening a menu without recognizing one word on it and the disappointment of being served something other than what you thought you'd ordered. On our first trip to Europe, we were served a plate of cold brains; we thought we had ordered chicken. This guide was created for the traveler who wants to enjoy, appreciate and experience authentic cuisine *and* know what he or she is eating.

The next time you find yourself seated in a red-tiled courtyard with the scent of simmering garlic in the night air and an incomprehensible menu in your hands, simply pull this guide from your pocket and get ready to enjoy the delicious cuisine of Italy.

In Italy and Ticino (the Italian-speaking region of Switzerland), the menu is almost always posted outside of the restaurant or in a window. This makes choosing a restaurant easy and fun as you "window shop" for your next meal.

Remember that the dish that you ordered may not be exactly as described in this guide. Every chef is (and should be) innovative. What we have listed for you in this guide is the most common version of a dish.

If a menu has an English translation it does not mean that the translation is correct. One travel writer, Margo Classé, (*Hello Italy!: An Insider's Guide to Italian Hotels $50-$90 A Night For Two*, ISBN 0-9653944-6-8, Wilson Publishing) once ordered beans and was served beets instead.

We recommend this guide for great budget hotels!

In Italy, it is customary to order a first course (pasta, rice or soup), a second course (meat, poultry or fish) and a side dish (salad, potato or vegetable). Rarely does an Italian order only a first course (such as ordering only pasta).

Tipping

A 10 to 15% service charge is almost always added to your bill (*il conto*) in Italy. Depending on the service, it is customary to leave an additional 5 to 10%. The menu will usually note that service is included (*servizio incluso* or *servizio compreso*). A service charge, by law, is included in all restaurant bills in Ticino.

You will often find *coperto* or cover charge on your menu (a small charge just for placing your butt at the table).

Mealtimes

In Northern Italy, lunch is served from noon to around 2 p.m., and dinner from 7 p.m. to 10 p.m. In the South, lunch is served from 1 p.m. and dinner from 8 p.m. No "early bird special" in Italy. Ticino's hours are the same as in Northern Italy.

Water

Europeans joke that you can tell a U.S. tourist from his fanny pack, clothes and ubiquitous bottle of mineral water. Tap water is safe in Italy and Switzerland. Occasionally, you will find *non potabile* signs in restrooms (especially in the rest stops of highways). This means that the water is not safe for drinking.

Waiters and waitresses will often bring *acqua minerale* (mineral water) to your table. You will be charged for it, so if you do not want mineral water ask for *acqua semplice* (tap water).

Types of Eating Establishments

Bacaro: Venetian wine bar serving snacks like Spanish *tapas*.

Bottiglieria: Simple drinking establishments with limited menus but plenty of bottles of wine. Originally, these "bottle shops" only served liquor. Also called *fiaschetteria*, *cantina* or *trani*.

Enoteca: Wine bar

Gelateria: Shop serving *gelato* (ice cream)

Grotto: Ticino has many *grotti*. These are village restaurants which take their name from caves used to store food and wine. Originally, a *grotto* was a simple eating establishment, but today many are quite expensive with extensive menus.

Locanda: Found in the country, serves regional meats and seafood.

Osteria: A tavern or wine shop. This name has also come to refer to a restaurant. These can also be called *cucina* or *hosteria*.

Pasticceria: Pastry shop

Panineria: Usually serves only sandwiches.

Pizzeria: We think you can figure this one out.

Ristorante: A restaurant

Roticceria: A deli, sometimes with a few tables, where you can order grilled meats.

Tavola Calda: Small restaurant with take-out or fast foods and usually with a few tables.

Trattoria: Less expensive family-run restaurant, usually not too fancy.

ITALY

ABRUZZO & MOLISE
(Off-the-Beaten-Track Italy)

Along the Adriatic coast are the
mountainous regions of Abruzzo
and Molise. The quiet hill towns
are in great contrast to the Adriatic
resorts. The most notable tourist venue
is the Abruzzo National Park, a place for
hikers and nature lovers. Outside this nature
reserve is Scanno, a popular summer resort
town. L`Aquila (which means "the eagle") is
the capital of Abruzzo and a business center.
Few tourists from the United States and
Canada visit this part of Italy. If you are
looking for off-the-beaten-track destinations and mountain scenery, Molise and
Abruzzo will certainly please.

Inland, you will find menus dominated by
capretto (baby goat), *agnello arrosto* (roast lamb), and
porchetta (roast pig). On the coast (in restaurants not
serving tourist fare) try *brodetto* (fish soup). *Centerbe*
(a green herb liquor) accompanies many meals. For
dessert, try *confetti* (flower-shaped candy made from sugar-
coated almonds).

APULIA (The "Heel" of Italy)

Apulia (Pulia) is the "heel" of Italy. Oppressively hot in July and
August, a rainy day is rare. Apulia is a large wine-producing

region. The area is not frequented by many North American tourists. The baroque town of Martina Franca and the white-washed town of Locorotondo are in the wine region and worth a visit. Part of the coast is heavily industrialized with immense steelworks. Bari is a modern port and a common departure point for travelers to Greece. An interesting architec-tural feature are the *trulli*, stone dome-shaped white-washed buildings. The largest collection of *trulli* are found near Alberobello. The Adriatic fishing ports have architecture similar to the old Venetian ports. Taranto is a modern town as is the important port of Brindisi, another frequent departure point for vis-its to Greece. Not to be missed is the lovely Baroque town of Lecce.

Friuli-Venezia Giulia

Veneto

San Marino

Le Marche

Abruzzo

Molise

Apulia

Campania

Basilicata

Calabria

Sicily

Focaccia barese (stuffed pizza), often with *burrata* (very buttery cheese), *triglia* (red mullet), *spigola* (sea bass), *orecchiette con le cime de rapa* (ear-shaped pasta with turnips) and *tiella di riso e cozze* (a mussels, rice and potato dish) can all be found on Apulia's menus. Some avoid the *polpi arricciati* ("curled octopus") when they see that the octopus is beaten and twirled in a basket in order to get the desired "curled" shape of the octopus. *Bianco di Martina* is a common fortified wine found in Apulia.

BASILICATA (Undiscovered Italy)

This area was once known as Lucania. One of Italy's smallest regions, Basilicata is also its poorest. Mountainous and barren, Basilicata is not visited by many tourists. The capital city of Potenza was badly damaged in a 1980's earthquake. The hill town of Maratea is dramatically situated on the coast. Here, in small villages such as Metaponto and Matera, you experience the simple Italy.

The spicy *sugna piccante* (pork sauce) flavors many dishes. *Maiale* (pork), is found on most menus and cured meats like the sausage *luganega*, *luganica* or *lucanica* (there are even more spellings than this!) are common. *Peperoncini* (small hot green peppers preserved in oil) are added to many dishes. Try *scamorza* cheese (the local version of aged *mozzarella*).

CALABRIA (The "Toe" of Italy)

Sun, white-sand beaches, rugged mountains, olive groves and the huge rock of Scilla are all found on the "toe" of Italy. The area was once known as Magna Graecia, and there are villages where a Greek dialect is still spoken. The mountain towns such as Serra San Bruno remain as they were several hundred years ago. Rossano is a beautiful medieval town overlooking a great ravine. Consenza is a town built on a steep hillside with an interesting (almost dilapidated) look to it. Many tourists find themselves in modern Reggio on their way to Sicily. The small towns of Pizzo and Tropea are worth a visit to experience the true Calabria. We would be remiss if we did not mention that some areas of Calabria are strongholds of the local mafia and not recommended for travel.

Costolette d'agnello (lamb chops) and *pesce spada* (swordfish) are found on most menus. *Novellame* is a spread of salted anchovies and *peperoncino* sauce. Pasta is often served with chickpeas (*ceci*). *Stracotto* is a beef stew which in Calabria includes carrots, mushrooms, onions, nutmeg and cloves. *Caviale de sud* or "caviar of the south" is a dish of fried fish preserved in oil and powdered with *peperoncino*. *Fichi* (figs) are featured in many desserts.

CAMPANIA (Naples, Capri & the Amalfi Coast)

Naples, in the shadow of Vesuvius, is congested, noisy, has a reputation as dangerous, and is not an easy city for the tourist. After a quick view of Naples' old town along the harbor, most head for the nearby ruins of Herculaneum and Pompeii. It is an eerie experience walking through nearly perfectly preserved ancient communities buried by the volcanic eruption of Vesuvius. The volcanic island of Ischia and nearby Capri are often overrun by day trippers in high season. Although it can be expensive, Capri (with its breathtaking vistas) remains the favorite of many returning visitors. The gateway to the Amalfi coast is Sorrento, perched over the sea. The Amalfi coast is the most spectacular coastal drive in Italy (if you have the nerve to drive it in high season). Positano has a great beach with a view of the town perched on the bluff. Amalfi and Ravello, further down the Amalfi coast, have spectacular views. The Amalfi coast reigns as one of the most scenic and photographed coasts in the world.

Along the coast, seafood is prevalent, especially *polpi affogati* (octopus in a spicy tomato sauce). Pizza, said to have originated in Naples, is found in many varieties. *Pizza alla Napoletana* is pizza with tomato sauce and anchovies. You will eat tomatoes here like you have never had before. Many pasta dishes are served *al pomodoro* (with a tomato sauce). Meat is often cooked *alla pizzaiola* (in a tomato sauce with garlic). *Partenopea* on a menu simply means served Naples style. For dessert try *sfogliatella* (flaky pastry filled with sweet *ricotta* cheese).

EMILIA-ROMAGNA (From the Adriatic Sea to Central Italy)

The Romans built a grand road from Rimini on the Adriatic Sea to Piacenza in central Italy. Along this road, the Via Emilia, developed the towns which now make up the Emilia-Romagna region. Piacenza is a major industrial city with a lovely downtown. Parma (which lends its name to the famous Parma ham or *prosciutto*), Modena (home to the Ferrari and Maserati automobiles), Bologna (a learning center and important Italian city for commerce) and Ferrara (less spoiled by modern times than the others) are all towns with important historic centers. Imposing Ravenna is in contrast to the most popular Adriatic resort of Rimini. Be careful, as Rimini can be quite dull, even completely closed, off season and extremely overcrowded in season.

The coast features *brodetto* (fish soup). *Prosciutto di Parma* (Parma ham) is common as is *risotto* (the famous Italian rice dish). Suckling pig is called *lattonzolo* here. For dessert, try *castagnole* (chestnut fritters). True Italian food is rare in Rimini, which has revised its menus to cater to the European package tourist.

FRIULI-VENEZIA GIULIA (Trieste & the Austrian Border)

This region borders on Austria and Slovenia. Udine is the capital but Trieste draws the most attention. Trieste, which remained under United Nations control until 1954, is an interesting mix of Austrian and Italian with a Slavic influence from the former

Yugoslav republics. The architecture along the port demonstrates the mix of rulers of Trieste. Our several trips to Trieste have made us realize that this area is often, unfortunately, overlooked by tourists. White wine is produced in the hills of Friuli-Venezia Giulia. Visit the towns of Colli Orientali and Collio. The small mountain towns along the Austrian border allow the visitor to experience a mixture of Italy and Austria.

Jota is a minestrone found here and usually contains sauerkraut. *Polenta* (cornmeal mush) is found everywhere. *Brodetto* (fish soup) is common in the coastal area of this region. *Cialzons* are sweet-and-sour pasta found here. The town of San Daniele is the home of *prosciutto di San Daniele* (a cured ham). The Slavic influence is found in the Trieste dessert of *gubana* (sweet bread roll) and the Austrian influence is found in the many coffeehouses of Trieste.

LAZIO (Rome & its Environs)

Lazio (also called Latium) is the region around Rome. To try to list Rome's main attractions would require another guide. Rome can be a frustrating city (it can be hard to carry on a conversation while walking down the street due to the constant traffic noise). But, difficulties aside, few places in the world have so many important sites in such a small area, including the Vatican with its Sistine Chapel, Circus Maximus, the Spanish Steps, the Trevi Fountain, the catacombs...

Sperlonga, San Felice Circeo, Santa Severa and Santa Marinella are all coastal towns worth a visit. Ostia is a large coastal city near Rome and was the main Roman port. Its impressive ruins are an easy day trip from Rome. In inland Lazio, you may visit Tivoli (with Hadrian's Villa), Palestrina, the mountain town of Subiaco and the walled town of Viterbo.

Rome is said to have 5,000 restaurants. In Rome, you can eat just about anything. After a gruelling day of site-seeing, stop in a small restaurant (*trattoria*), drink some wine and eat a hearty dish of pasta such as one served *alla arrabbiata* (in a spicy tomato and herb sauce) or *alla carbonara* (with bacon, cheese, olive oil and eggs). Meals often start with *bruschetta* (garlic toast) and end with *grappa* (of which we had a little too much on our first night in Rome). When in Rome...

LE MARCHE (The Apennines Mountain Region)

The Apennines Mountains separate Le Marche from the rest of Central Italy. Ancona, on the Adriatic coast (a common departure point for Venice) is a modern port town. Pilgrims visit the house of the Virgin Mary in Loreto (brought to this sight, according to legend, by angels). Urbino, one of the lesser-known great Renaissance cities, looks much like it did in the fifteenth century. In the Tronto River Valley, scenic Ascoli Piceno is another Le Marche town worth visiting. Most travelers head for the crowded (package-tour-filled) coastal towns. These crowded resorts are in great contrast to the sedate hill towns.

Truffles (*tartufi*) are a specialty here and summer peaches (*pesche*) and plums (*susine*) are some of the best fruits you will ever taste. *Vincigrassi* (baked lasagna dish), *olive all'ascolana* (large stuffed olives), *porchetta* (roast suckling pig) and rabbit (*coniglio)* are popular. *Brodetto di pesce* (fish soup) is found along the coast. In Ancona, *brodetto* contains thirteen varieties of fish.

LIGURIA (The Italian Riviera)

Wedged between mountains and the sea, the coastal region of Liguria stretches from the French border to Tuscany and is a popular tourist destination. Genoa, a large industrial city, is also Italy's biggest port. Tourists usually visit only the old, central part of the city. West of Genoa toward the French border are the bright tourist towns of Ventimiglia and Bordighera. San Remo (with its famous casino) is the largest resort. East from Genoa, you will find the resort of Nervi with beautiful parks. Further down the coast are the resort towns of Camogli, Rapallo, Santa Margherita and of course, perhaps the best known and most beautiful Italian port of Portofino. One drawback is the gridlock in and out of Portofino in high season. Sestri Levante makes a good base for exploring the highlight of any trip to Liguria, the Cinque Terre, five beautiful towns, which until recently were accessible only by train or a series of hiking paths. Perched on dramatic cliffs above the sea, you will experience carless serenity and an Italy of old. Down the coast is Lerici (where we had one of our most memorable meals in an open-air restaurant on the port).

Seafood is dominant in Liguria, especially *branzino* (sea bass), *aragosta* (lobster), *vongole* (clams), *zuppa di datteri* (fish soup), *stoccafisso* (dried cod), *ciuppin* (fish and vegetable stew) and *fritto misto di frutti di mare* (mixed seafood, usually grilled). Sadly, seafood is becoming less common because of pollution and overfishing in the Mediterranean. *Basilico* (basil) grown in the hills above the sea forms the basis of *pesto* and is common in the cuisine of Liguria. Try *ravioli di magro* (pasta stuffed with herbs and *ricotta* cheese).

LOMBARDY (Milan & the Lake District)

Fashionable, modern Milan is an important center of Italian commerce. If you like to shop, Milan is the place. Tourists often visit four important sites: the Duomo (cathedral, especially the ornate roof), La Scala (the opera house), the Last Supper and the Galleria Vittorio Emanuele (the famous glass-domed shopping center).

In great contrast to Milan is the Lake District, including Lakes Orta (often, regrettably, ignored), Maggiore, Como, and Garda. The towns that line these lakes remain dotted with former palaces (many now resorts) with impressive formal gardens. Many believe the Lake District is Italy at its best. On Lake Como, Bellagio is the most famous resort, but Varenna, with its tiny harbor and splendid beach, is the favorite of many.

Trota (trout) is popular in the Lake District. Lombardy specialties include *stracotto* (pot roast), *ossobuco* (braised veal shank) and *capretto* (roast kid). You will find many dishes served *alla milanese* (battered with eggs and breadcrumbs and fried). *Riso alla milanese* is a popular rice dish with a golden color from the ingredient saffron. *Gorgonzola* (a delicious blue cheese) is often found in pasta dishes. Lombardy cheeses also included *crescenza* (a soft, buttery cheese) and *mascarpone* (a very creamy cheese). *Torrone* (honey and almond nougat) is a common dessert.

PIEDMONT & VALLE D'AOSTA (Turin & the Alps)

Sometimes the Alpine regions of Piedmont (which means "foot of the mountain") and Valle d'Aosta (north of Piedmont) feel more like France or Switzerland than Italy. Valle d'Aosta has two official languages: Italian and French. Many come to the largest city in these regions, Turin (Torino), to see the Shroud of Turin (believed by some to be the cloth in which Christ's body was wrapped after the crucifixion). North of Turin, into Valle d'Aosta, is Saint Vincent (a popular gambling resort). Any trip to this area would not be complete without a visit to Breuil-Cervina at the base of the Matterhorn (Monte Cervino) with breath-taking views of this famous mountain peak. Courmayeur, another Alpine resort, is the gateway to Mont Blanc (Monte Bianco) on the French border. The walled city of Aosta is nestled in the Alps. Asti (yes, as in the wine), Novara, Vercelli, and Casale Monferrato are all towns with impressive medieval towers. If you are looking for beautiful mountain scenery, don't miss these regions.

Piemontese on a menu means "Piedmont style" or with white truffles. *Tartufi bianchi* are famous white truffles from Alba and Asti. *Alla Valdostana* on a menu means "Valle d'Aosta style" and usually means with ham and cheese. Roast game, sausages and butter play heavy roles in the local diet. *Tajarin* is thin ribbon pasta made golden with egg yolks. *Fonduta* (fondue) is popular. The French influence can be found in *crespelle* (crêpes). You will find *cervo* (venison), *carbonade* (beef cooked in wine and onions) and *arrosto misto* (grilled meats) here along with *trota* (trout). *Gianduiotti* are hazelnut chocolates found in Turin and one of our favorite treats. *Torta di nocciole*, hazelnut cake, is a must.

SAN MARINO (Europe's Oldest Country)

With about only 25,000 people and 24 square miles, San Marino (totally surrounded by Italy) claims to be Europe's oldest existing country. San Marino's official name is the Most Serene Republic of San Marino, and is located 15 miles inland from the Adriatic Sea resort of Rimini. Its chief industries are tourism and the sale of postage stamps. Mt. Titano, upon which San Marino sits, must be climbed after you leave your car. There are three medieval fortresses on the mountain. The capital, also named San Marino, is a maze of attractive narrow streets.

Food is typical Italian. You'll find *coniglio* (rabbit) and *nidi di rondine* (pasta rolls). Don't miss *caciatella* (San Marino's version of crème caramel).

SARDINIA (SARDEGNA)

The island of Sardinia is located about 115 miles off the western coast of Italy in the Mediterranean. Ten miles to the north is the French island of Corsica. Sardinia has been a part of Italy since 1861. Cagliari, the capital, is on the south coast, which is known for its ancient ruins. For the most part, Sardinia remains unspoiled from its rocky coast to its mountainous interior. The northeastern Costa Smeralda (Emerald Coast) is the only area where tourist development has arrived. Those looking for peace and quiet and even isolation should experience the mountainous inland region of Barbagia.

Lobster (*aragosta*) is plentiful along the coast, and the northern coast of Sardinia is sometimes referred to as the lobster coast. Lamb (*agnello*), rabbit (*cunillu*) and trout (*trota*) are ubiquitous. Grilled meats are a specialty. The shepherds of Sardinia have feasted on *pane carasau*, which is also known as *carta da musica* (music paper). Durham wheat, salt, water and yeast are the simple ingredients for this wood-fire-baked bread. You will find this thin, crispy bread used as a pizza crust.

Other specialties of Sardinia include *porceddu* (roast suckling pig which is the "national" dish of Sardinia), *cascà* (couscous) and many honey-based desserts such as *sebadas* (deep-fried cheese-filled ravioli soaked in honey).

French, Arabs, Spanish and Italians have all controlled Sicily, the largest and most populated island in the Mediterranean. Travelers will find some of the best-preserved Greek and Roman ruins here along with the ornate architecture of its churches and palaces. Agrigento is the home to the most important archaeological site in Sicily, the Greek "Valley of the Temples." Siracusa (Syracuse) is also known for its Greek and Roman ruins. The capital is Palermo, but most travelers head to the medieval town of Taormina on the east coast in the shadows of Mount Etna, an active volcano. Messina (destroyed by both an earthquake and the bombs of World War II) has bland, modern architecture and is in strong contrast to the picturesque fishing port of Cefalù.

Sicilian cuisine is not simply pasta and olive oil but incorporates Italian, Greek, French, Spanish and Arab influences. Some specialties are *pasta con le sarde* (pasta with fresh sardines), *pesce spada* (swordfish), and the simple *cicina* (a mixture of fried small fish). Other specialties are *caponata* (sweet-and-sour sauce with eggplant, tomatoes, onions and peppers), *pasta alla Norma* (pasta with a tomato, basil and eggplant sauce topped with *ricotta* cheese) and *costoletta alla siciliana* (thin slices of veal or beef topped with chopped garlic and *parmesan* cheese, then breaded and deep-fried).

Desserts, and Sicilians are famous for their desserts, include *cannoli* (pastry tubes filled with sweetened *ricotta* cheese) and *cassata alla siciliana* (layered sponge cake).

Marsala wine (from the town of the same name) is a fortified wine which can range from rich and sweet to dry.

TICINO (Italian-Speaking Switzerland)

Ticino is the main Italian-speaking canton or region of
Switzerland. Palm trees, Italian architecture, Swiss orderliness and
Italian food all make Ticino (with its famous resorts of Lugano
and Locarno) a great travel destination. Ticino is Switzerland's
southernmost canton, bordering on Italy, and has been a part of
Switzerland since the early 1800's. This region has always
remained strongly Italian. Italian is one of four official languages
of Switzerland (along with French, German and Romansh).

Specialties found in Ticino are *risotto ai fiori di zucca* (a rice dish
made with a heavy cream base and zucchini flowers stirred in along
with *parmesan* cheese), *pancetta arrotolata* (rolled bacon flavored
with cloves), *capretto* (baby goat), *fritto misto* (breaded and fried
lake fish), *cotto antico* (bay leaf-flavored salami) and *giambonetti di
pollo* (stuffed chicken leg). Bread is a staple in all meals, especially
bread with a thick crust dusted with flour called *crusca*. Two common cheeses found in Ticino are *formaggini di capra* (fresh goat's-
milk cheese) and *formaggini d'Alpe* (a common cow's-milk cheese).
Both of these cheeses are eaten with olive oil, salt and pepper.

TRENTINO-ALTO ADIGE (The Dolomites)

The Alto Adige is the far north of Italy and is more like Austria than
Italy. The Dolomite Mountains dominate this area. At the Brenner
Pass, on the border with Austria, is the town of Bolzano/Bozen
(Austrian until 1918). Near Bolzano is the wine town of Caldaro.
Bressanone/Brixen is a beautiful mountain town and the Alto Adige's
oldest city. Ortisei, San Martino and Madonna di Campiglio are all
both summer and winter resort towns. Breathtaking views abound in
Brunico/Bruneck. Merano has an interesting old town and famous
spas. Trento, the capital of Trentino, is more Italian than Austrian

and remains an attractive and architecturally interesting town.

Food here is more German than Italian (especially the farther north you travel). Game, dumplings (*knoedel*) and cured ham (*speck*) all stress the German influence. Sauerkraut (*crauti*) is featured heavily in dishes as are *wurstel* (hot dogs and brats). For dessert, apples, grown in large numbers in the region, are often added to the Germanic dessert of *strudel*

TUSCANY (One of the World's Most Popular Destinations)

There are so many picturesque towns in Tuscany, space allows only a few highlights. With unspoiled hills, perfectly preserved towns and great food and wine, Tuscany is one of the most popular tourist destinations in Italy and the world. Since childhood, we wanted to see the Leaning Tower of Pisa (and the nearby and lesser known baptistry). Too bad there are so many hawkers of plastic leaning towers all over Pisa. Siena's main square, the Piazza de Campo, and ornate cathedral are only two gems in the beautiful town with (thankfully) a car-free center. San Gimignano, with its walls and towers, is an incredibly picturesque town. The hilltop towns of Lucca, Montepulciano, Montalcino and Pienza are all worth a visit. Of course, Florence is the favorite of many visitors to Italy. Its wealth of art, housed in buildings which themselves are art, leaves many visitors wanting to return again and again.

Start your meal with *crostini* (toasted bread with various toppings). *La bistecca all Fiorentina*, a T-bone steak, must not be missed nor should any number of the *pecorino* cheeses. Menus often include *cinghiale* (wild boar), and dishes served *alla lepre* (in a rabbit-based sauce), *arista* (roast, seasoned pork loin) and *ribollita* (bean and/or cabbage soup which means "twice-cooked soup). *Chianti*, *chianti* and more *chianti*. Enough said!

Green hills, towns spared from industrialization, and wonderful dining combine to make Umbria an outstanding Italian destination (especially by car). Perugia is Umbria's largest city with a historic city center, but most tourists come here to visit the smaller towns like Gubbio in northern Umbria. Orvieto is located on a monumental square-shaped rock visible for miles. Don't miss this impressive and well-preserved town (or a sip or much more of its famous wines). Assisi is home of a huge basilica built in memory of local hero St. Francis. It is ironic that such a huge basilica was built for such a humble man or that the streets are filled with St. Francis key chains. Still, Assisi, perched on a hill, is a memorable sight. Walled Spoleto (home of the well-known art festival) is dominated by a large castle and stationed in wooded countryside.

Tartufi (truffles) are a specialty here, especially the black truffle (*tartufo nero*). *Stringozzi* (homemade pasta) is used in many dishes, especially in Spoleto. *Strozzapreti* (dumplings with meat sauce) is a dish with the strange name of "priest stranglers" after a priest allegedly choked on it. *Palombacci* are small songbirds cooked whole on a spit. For dessert, try *stinchetti* (marzipan cakes). Of course, no one thinks of eating in Umbria without drinking one of the many fine wines of this region.

VENETO (Venice & its Environs)

Veneto is the region around Venice. Despite the tourists, the sometimes smelly canals and the often inflated prices, Venice is unlike anywhere else in the world. Many cities claim to be pedestrian only, but Venice is truly car-free. Don't just take a day trip here. Once the day trippers leave, Venice becomes a quiet, romantic maze of streets with spectacular architecture. As many times as we have visited, we are always amazed at the splendid beauty of Venice with its buildings rising out of the sea. Don't miss the Piazza San Marco, the Bridge of Sighs, the Basilica di San Marco and the Doge's Palace. If time permits, visit the islands of Murano (famous for its ornate glass), Burano (famous for its lace), San Michele (Venice's island cemetery) and Torcello (for a taste of an almost deserted island).

Veneto includes the cities of Vicenza, Padua (where you can see the "uncorrupted" tongue of St. Anthony), Verona and Treviso. Many towns remain unspoiled and rarely visited by tourists, including Valpolicella (home of this popular Italian red wine) and the hills of Colli Euganei (home of hot thermal springs) and Asolo. North of Treviso are the mountain resorts of Cortina d' Ampezzo and Belluno.

Cape sante (scallops), *baccalà* (dried cod), *fegato alla veneziana* (liver with onions), *seppie* (cuttlefish) and *granseola* (crab) are all specialties of Venice. *Polenta* (the famous cornmeal mush) is found throughout the region. *Carpaccio* is thinly sliced raw beef served in a sauce and was named by the owner of Harry's Bar in Venice after a famous Venetian painter. *Prosecco* is a slightly sparkling wine from Veneto and worth a try. While in Venice, don't miss having an evening drink or *caffè* in the Piazza San Marco.

Speaking Italian - Pronunciation Guide

If you are looking for a comprehensive guide to speaking Italian, this is not the the place. These are simply a few tips for speaking Italian followed by a very brief pronunciation guide. It is always good to learn a few polite terms so that you can excuse yourself when you've stepped on the foot of an elderly lady or spilled your drink down the back of the gentleman in front of you. It's also just common courtesy to greet the people you meet in your hotel, in shops and restaurants in their own language.

In Italian, you pronounce every letter. E and i are soft vowels when used with consonants. The final e is always pronounced.

The second to the last syllable is stressed. If there is an accent in the word, stress the accented syllable.

a like in father.
au like ow in bow.
b the same as in English.
c **ca, co** and **cu** like k in keep.
– **ce** and **ci**, like ch in cheap.
ch like k in kite.
d the same as in English.
e like in day.
ei like ay in lay.
f the same as in English.
g **ga, go** and **gu** like g in gate.
ge and **gi** like j in jar.
gh like g in goat.
gl like gl in glow except before i, then like lli in million.
gn like ni in onion.
h silent. H after a consonant gives it a hard sound.

i like ee in jeep.
ie, io, iu, **i** is pronounced as a y (ie. *pensione* ~ pen syo neh).
k/l/m/n the same as in English.
o usually like o in boat.
p/q the same as in English.
ue, ui, uo, the u is pronounced like a w (ie. *buono* ~ bwo no).
r with a slight trill.
s like s in sit except between two vowels, then like s in hose.
sc **sca, sco** or **scu** as sk in skirt. **sce** or **sci** as sh in sharp.
t the same as English.
u like oo in foot.
v the same as in English.
z the same as ds in fads.

English to Italian

This is a brief listing of some familiar English food and food-related words that you may need in a restaurant, followed by a list of phrases that may come in handy.

anchovy, acciuga (acciughe)

appetizer, antipasto (i)

apple, mela (e)

artichoke, carciofo (i)

ashtray, portacenere

asparagus, asparago (i)

bacon, pancetta

baked, al forno

banana, banana (e)

bean, fagiolo (i)

beef, manzo (di bue)

beefsteak, bistecca (di manzo)

beer, birra (e)

beverage, bevanda (e)

bill, conto (i)

bitter, amaro (a)

boiled, bollito/lesso

bottle, bottiglia

bowl, scodella

bread, pane

bread rolls, panino (i)

breakfast, prima colazione

broiled, graticola/griglia

broth, brodo

butter, burro

cabbage, cavolo (i)

cake, torta (e)

candle, candela

carrot, carota (e)

cereal, cereale (i)

chair, sedia

check, conto (i)

cheers, salute/cin cin

cheese, formaggio (formaggi)

cherry, ciliegia (e)

chicken soup, brodo di pollo/zuppa di pollo

chicken, pollo

chop, costoletta (e)

clam, vongola (e)

cocktail, cocktail

cod, baccalà/merluzzo

coffee, caffè (also black coffee)

coffee w/hot water (to dilute), caffè amercano

coffee w/milk, caffè latte

coffee (decaf), caffè hag/caffè decaffeinato

coffee w/cream, caffè con panna

cold, freddo (a)

corn, mais

cover charge, pane coperto

cucumber, cetriolo (i)

cup, coppa

   tazza coffee/tea cup

custard, crema

dessert, dolce (i)

dinner, cena
dish (plate), piatto
drink, bevanda (e)
dry (as in wine), secco
duck, anitra/anatra
egg, uovo (a)
espresso, caffè espresso
fish, pesce
fish soup, zuppa di pesce
fork, forchetta
french fries, patate fritte
fresh, fresco (a)
fried, fritto (a)/fritti (e)
fruit, frutta
game, cacciagione/selvaggina
garlic, aglio
gin, gin
glass, bicchiere
grapefruit, pompelmo
grape, uva (e)
green bean, fagiolino (i)
grilled, griglia or alla griglia
half, mezzo (a)
ham (cooked), prosciutto cotto
ham (cured), prosciutto crudo
hamburger, hamburger
honey, miele
hors d'oeuvre, antipasto
hot, caldo (a)
iced, ghiacciato
ice coffee, caffè freddo
ice cream, gelato (i)

ice (on the rocks), ghiaccio
    or con ghiaccio
ice water, acqua fredda
iced tea, tè freddo
ketchup, ketchup/salsa di
    pomodoro
knife, coltello
lamb, abbacchio/agnello
large, grande
lemon, limone (i)
lettuce, lattuga
little (a little), un pó
liver, fegato (fegatini)
lobster, aragosta (e)
loin, lombata
lunch, pranzo
marinated, marinato (a)
match, fiammifero (i)
meat, carne
medium (cooked), a puntino
    or normale
melon, melone
menu, carta or menù
milk, latte
mineral water, acqua minerale
mineral water (sparkling),
    acqua minerale gasata
**mineral water (w/out
carbonation),** acqua
    minerale non gasata
mixed, mista (o)
mushroom, fungo (i)

mussel, cozza (e)

mustard, senape

napkin, tovagliolo

noodles, taglierini/pasta

octopus, polipo/polpo

oil, olio

olive oil, olio d'oliva

omelette, frittata

on the rocks (w/ ice), con ghiaccio

onion, cipolla (e)

orange, arancia (arance)

orange juice, succo d'arancia

overdone, ben cotto

oyster, ostrica (ostriche)

pastries, dolci/paste

peach, pesca (pesche)

pear, pera (e)

pea, pisello (i)

pepper (black), pepe

pepper (bell), peperone (i)

perch, pesce persico

pineapple, ananas

plate (dish), piatto

please, per piacere

plum, susina (e)

poached, affogato

pork, maiale

potato, patata (e)

poultry, pollame

prawn, gamberetto (i)

rabbit, coniglio

rare, al sangue

raspberry, lampone (i)

receipt, ricevuta/scontrino

rice, riso

roast, arrosto

salad, insalata

salt, sale

sandwich, sandwich/panino (i)

sauce, salsa

saucer, piattino/sottocoppa

sautéed, saltato (i)/saltata (e)

scallops, cappe sante

scrambled, strapazzate

seafood, frutti di mare

seasoning, condimento (i)

shrimp, scampo (i), gamberetto (i)

small, piccolo (i)/piccola (e)

smoked, affumicata (o)

snail, lumaca (lumache)

sole, sogliola (e)

soup, zuppa (e)/minestra (e)

spaghetti, spaghetti

sparkling wine, spumante

specialty, specialità

spinach, spinaci

spoon, cucchiaio

squid, calamaro (i)

steak, bistecca

steamed, a vapore

stewed, in umido

strawberry, fragola (e)

sugar, zucchero
sugar substitute, dolcificante
supper, cena
sweet, dolce
table, tavolo
tea, tè
tea w/lemon, tè al limone
tea w/milk, tè al latte
teaspoon, cucchiaino
thank you, grazie
tip, mancia
toasted, tostato
tomato, pomodoro (i)
trout, trota
tumbler (glass), bicchiere
tuna, tonno
turkey, tacchino
utensil, posata (e)/utensile (i)
veal, vitello
veal scallop, scaloppa di vitello
vegetable, legume (i).
  Verdura (e) green vegetables
vegetarian, vegetariana (o)
venison, carne di cervo
vinegar, aceto
waiter, cameriere
waitress, cameriera
water, acqua
well done, ben cotto
whipped creme, panna montata
wine, vino
wine (full-bodied), vino corposo

wine list, lista dei vini
wine (red), vino rosso
wine (rosé), vino rosé
wine (white), vino bianco

Prego, can mean: thank you, you're welcome, this way (with a hand gesture), please, okay, and can I help you.

C*iao* means hello *and* goodbye.

Italians answer the phone with *Pronto?*

please, per piacere/per favore
thank you, grazie
yes, sì
no, no
good morning, buon giorno
good afternoon/evening, buona sera
good night, buona notte
goodbye, arrivederci/ciao
Do you speak English?, Parla inglese?
I don't speak Italian, Non parlo italiano
excuse me, mi scusi (or *scusi*)
I don't understand, non capisco
I'm hungry, Ho fame
I'm thirsty, Ho sete

I'd like..., Vorrei...

I'd like a table, please, Vorrei un tavolo, per piacere

I want to reserve a table, Vorrei riservare un tavolo

for one person, per uno (una)

for two persons, per due tre (3), quattro (4), cinque (5), sei (6), sette (7), otto (8), nove (9), dieci (10)

this evening, stasera

tomorrow, domani

the day after tomorrow, dopodomani

near the window, vicino alla finestra

outside, fuori

inside, dentro

on the patio, sulla veranda

no smoking, zona per non fumatori

where is?, dov'è

the bathroom, il bagno/ la toilette

The bill please, il conto, per piacere

a mistake, errore

Is service included?, E' incluso il servizio?

Do you accept credit cards?, Posso pagare con una carta di credito?

How much does this cost?, Quanto costa?

What is this?, Cos' è questo?

This is not what I ordered, Non ho ordinato questo

This is, Questo è...

too, troppo

a little, un po'

cold, freddo (a)

hot, caldo (a)

spicy, piccante

not fresh, non è fresco

undercooked, troppo crudo

overcooked, troppo cotto/ stracotto

very good, molto buono

delicious, delizioso (a)

diet, dieta

closed, chiuso (a)

monday, lunedì

tuesday, martedì

wednesday, mercoledì

thursday, giovedì

friday, venerdì

saturday, sabato

sunday, domenica

Words and letters in parentheses indicate plurals.

abbacchio, lamb

abbacchio alla cacciatora, pieces of lamb braised w/rosemary, garlic, wine & peppers

abboccato, a medium-sweet wine

abbrustolito, toasted

abruzzese, red pepper sauce

acciuga (acciughe), anchovy

acciughe al limone, anchovies w/lemon-based sauce

Words that end in A or O are singular

acerbo, sour

aceto, vinegar

aceto balsamico, balsamic vinegar. Aged vinegar used in many dishes, especially salads

Words that end in E or I are plural

acetosella, sorrel

acido, sour

acini di pepe, pasta for soup in the shape of peppercorns

acqua, water

acqua brillante, tonic water

acquacotta, bread & vegetable soup

acquadella, small whitebait fish

acqua dei rubinetto, tap water

acqua di seltz, seltzer water/soda water

"Acqua cotta" means cooked water

acqua fredda, ice water

acqua gasata, carbonated water

acqua ghiacciata, ice water

acqua minerale, mineral water

acqua minerale frizzante, extremely carbonated water

acqua minerale naturale, mineral water w/out carbonation

acqua naturale, tap water

acqua non gasata, water w/out carbonation

"Acqua del Rubinetto" is safe to drink but can taste weird. We usually order bottled water with meals.

acqua non potabile, do not drink the water!

acqua semplice, tap water

acqua tonica, tonic water

Acquavite, brandy/distilled spirit flavored w/caraway

affettato, sliced

affettato (i), cold cut

affogato, poached. This can also refer to ice cream soaked in coffee or liqueur

affumicato, smoked

agliata/all'aglio, garlic sauce

aglio, garlic

aglio e olio, w/garlic & olive oil

agnello, lamb

agnello alla turca, lamb stew w/raisins

agnolotti, filled pasta (square shaped)

Aglio.

agone, freshwater fish found in the lake country (the size of sardines)

agresto, juice of unripened grapes

agro, lemon juice & olive oil dressing

agrodolce, sweet & sour sauce

ai/al/all'/alla, in the style of/with

ajula, sea bream

ala, wing

alaccia, large sardine

Agresto is sometimes used in place of vinegar

alalunga, albacore (a type of tuna)

Albana, dry to semi-sweet wine from Emilia-Romagna

albicocca (albicocche), apricot

albume, egg white

alcolica, alcoholic. *Una bevanda alcolica* is an alcoholic beverage

alcool, alcohol

Aleatico, dessert wine (made from muscat grapes)

alette, wing

alfabetini, alphabet noodles for soup

al forno, baked

alfredo, w/butter & cream sauce

al fresco, outside (in the fresh air)

alice (i), anchovy

allodola (e), lark

alloro, bay leaf

ALLORO.

amabile, slightly sweet wine

amarena (e), sour cherry

amaretti, macaroons

amaretto, sweet almond-flavored liqueur

amaro, bitter/bitter cordial (bitters)

amatriciana, bacon, tomato & spices sauce

amburghese/amburgo, hamburger/ground meat

amburghese alla tirolese, hamburger served w/onion rings

Americano, Campari, vermouth & lemon peel

ammiru, prawns in Sicily

analcolico (i), non-alcoholic

ananas, pineapple

anatra, duck

anatroccolo, duckling

anelli/anellini, small circular pasta for soup (ring pasta)

aneto, dill

anguidda, another name for eel in Sicily

anguilla (e), eel.

anguilla alla veneziana, eel braised
    w/tuna & lemon sauce

In Perugia Anguilla can also refer to an eel shaped pastry created originally by nuns.

anguria, watermelon

anice, anise

animelle, sweetbreads

animelle alla salvia, sweetbreads w/sage

anisetta, anise-flavored liquor

anitra, duck

anitra germano, mallard duck

anitra selvatica, wild duck

annegati, slices of meat in wine

antipasto (i), appetizer

**antipasto alla marinara/antipasto di mare/antipasto di
pesce,** assorted seafood

antipasto misto, assorted appetizers

aperitivo, aperitif

arachide (i), peanut

      aragosta (e), lobster (crayfish)

34

arancia (i), orange. *Al arancia* means w/orange juice

aranciata, orangeade/orange soda

arancini, deep-fried rice balls

arancio di riso, cooked ball of rice stuffed w/meat & breaded & fried. This gets its name from the orange size of the ball

argentina, argentine fish

arigusta, crawfish

aringa, herring

aringa affumicata, smoked herring

arista, roast, seasoned pork loin

arista alla fiorentina, roasted pork rubbed w/garlic paste, cloves, salt, rosemary, pepper

arista di maiale/arista di suino, pork loin

arrabbiata, al, w/a spicy tomato & herb sauce

arrostetti, small roast

arrosti misti freddi, a selection of cold roasted meats

arrostini, veal chops

arrostino, small roast

arrostino annegato, small veal roast served with mushrooms

arrostite, grilled/roasted

arrosto/arrostito, roast/roasted

arrosto alla genovese, a roast w/onions, mushrooms & tomatoes

arrosto alla montanara, pot roast

arrosto con pastine, roast w/dough crust

arrosto di manzo, roast beef

arrosto in porchetta, roast suckling pig stuffed w/garlic, bacon & herbs

arrosto misto, mixed roast meats

arrosto morto, pot roast

arsella (e), mussel

asciutta (o), dry. Also refers to pasta w/sauce (as opposed to pasta for soup)

asiago, sharp cheese (round-shaped cheese)

asiago dolce, mild *asiago*

asparago (i), asparagus

asparago alla bismark, asparagus w/melted butter & fried egg

asparago alla milanese/asparago all'uovo, asapagus topped w/melted butter, *parmesan* cheese & fried egg

assortito (i), assorted

astice (i), prawn/lobster

Asti Spumante, sparkling white wine

attorta, fruit & almond-filled pastry

Aurum, orange liqueur

avvoltino, standing roast or rolled roast

babà, sponge cake covered w/rum

babaluci, snails in tomato & onion sauce

bacca (e), berry

baccalà, salt cod

baccalà alla fiorentina, salt cod floured & fried in oil & tomato sauce

baccalà alla lucana, salt cod cooked w/peppers

baccalà alla vicentina, salt cod w/onion, parsley, garlic, anchovies & cinnamon

bacio, chocolate hazelnut (means "kiss")

bagna cauda/bagna caoda, hot vegetable dip w/anchovies

bagnet, sauce (in Piedmont)

balsamella, bechamel/white sauce

banana (e), banana *Good Guess!*

barbabietola (e), beet

Barbaresco, soft red wine from Piedmont (lighter & drier than *Barolo*)

Barbera, dry red wine

barbe rosse, beets

Bardolino, pale, light red wine

Barolo, rich red wine from Piedmont

basilico, basil

bastoncini, bread sticks (means "little sticks")

battuta scanello, pounded round steak

battutina al prosciutto, hamburger mixed w/cured ham

battuto, finely chopped herbs, onions, celery & carrots

battuto di manzo, ground beef

bavette (i), thin, flat pasta

beccaccia, woodcock
beccaccino, snipe (game)
beccafico, warbler/song bird
belga, Belgian endive
bellini, sparkling wine & peach juice
bel paese, smooth, mild & soft cheese
ben cotta, well done
bensone, lemon cake
besciamella, white cream sauce
bevanda (e), drink/beverage
bevanda compresa, cost of drinks included
bianchetti, small anchovy (or sardine)
bianchi, white
bianco, white wine
Bianco di Martina, a fortified wine found in Apulia
bianco, in, w/butter (w/out a sauce)
bibita (e), drink/beverage
bibite analcoliche, soft drinks
bicchiere, glass
biete, Swiss chard
bietole, beet/Swiss chard
bietole alla padella, Swiss chard cooked w/butter &/or oil
bietoline, beet greens
bietolini, Swiss chard
bignè/bignole (con crema), cream puff
bigoli, larger form of spaghetti
biova/biovetta, round bread loaf
birra, beer
birra alla spina, tap beer
birra analcolica, no-alcohol beer
birra bionda, light beer
birra chiara, light beer (lager)
birra di barile, draft beer
birra importata, imported beer
birra in bottiglia, bottled beer

*"Bel Paese"
means
beautiful
country*

Bicchiere.
BEE·KEE·AY·RAY

birra in lattina, beer in a can
birra scura, dark beer
biscotto (i), cookie/biscuit/cracker/sponge cake
biscotti di prato, cookies w/pieces of almond
biscuit tortoni, dessert of beaten egg whites & macaroon
  crumbs topped w/whipped cream & toasted almonds
bismark, alla, usually means served w/a fried egg
bistecca, steak
bistecca alla bismark, fried steak w/an egg on top
bistecca alla fiorentina, T-bone steak
bistecca alla pizzaiola, steak w/tomato & garlic sauce
bistecca di manzo, beef steak
bistecca di vitello, veal scallop
bistecca Fiorentina, T-bone steak
bistecca impanata, cutlet/chop
bistecche, steaks
bistecchine, thin steaks
bitto, firm, smoked cheese
bobe, sea bream
boccolotti, short tubular pasta
bocconcini, diced veal w/tomato & white wine sauce/
  mozzarella balls
boldro, monkfish in Tuscany
boletus, porcini mushrooms
bollito (i), boiled. Can also mean
  meat or fish stew
bollito di gallina, boiled chicken
bollito di manzo, boiled beef
bollito misto, mixed boiled meats
bolognese, alla, usually means a tomato & meat sauce
bomba di riso, rice dish w/ground meat & herb fillings
bombolone (i), doughnut
bonèt, chocolate cream dessert. A specialty in Piedmont
borlotti, type of bean
boscaiola, means "woodsman style" & can refer to many
  things, including w/wild mushrooms
bosega, mullet

[handwritten note:] Bistecca Impanata is often breaded and fried in butter

[handwritten note:] "bocconcini" means mouthful

38

botolo, mullet

bottarga, fish eggs (tuna roe that has been salted & pressed)

bottiglia, bottle

bove, beef

bovoletti/bovoloni, small snails in Venice

brace, alla, on charcoal

braciola (e), rib steak/chop/cutlet

braciola di maiale, pork chop

bracioletta, small slice of meat

bracioletta a scottadito, lamb chops (charcoal grilled)

bracioline/braciolone, meat roll

braciolone alla napoletana, breaded steak, rolled & stewed

brandy, brandy

branzino, bass

branzinotti, small sea bass

brasato, braised/braised meat w/wine

bresaola, thinly sliced cured raw beef

briciole di pane, breadcrumbs

brioche, buns/rolls/small loaf (used for breakfast)

broccoletti, broccoli

broccoletti di rape, turnip greens

broccoletti strascinati, broccoli sautéed w/garlic & bacon

broccolo (i), broccoli

brodetto, rich fish soup

brodo, broth/soup/bouillon.
In brodo means cooked in broth

brodo di manzo, consomme/beef broth

brodo di pollo, chicken soup

brogue, sea bream

brovada, marinated turnips w/pork sausage

Brunello, full-bodied red wine from Montalcino

bruschetta, grilled bread w/garlic & olive oil (frequently topped w/tomatoes &/or onions)

brut, very dry wine

brutti, small almond cakes

bucaniera, tomato, garlic & seafood sauce

Broccolo.

Bucaniera...
Buccaneer,
get it?
Sea food Sauce.

bucatini, hollow spaghetti noodles

bucatoni, same as *bucatini*, but larger

budino, custard/pudding

budino alla toscana, cream cheese w/raisins, almonds, sugar & egg yolks

bue, beef

burrata, a very buttery cheese found in Apulia

burrida, fish stew or casserole. In Sardinia this refers to a poached & marinated fish dish

burrini, a type of hard, aged cheese

burro, butter

burro maggiordomo, butter w/lemon juice & parsley

busecca, tripe & vegetable soup

buttiri, a type of hard, aged cheese

cacao, cocoa

cacasor cioccolata, cocoa

cacciagione, game

cacciatora, alla/cacciatore, w/mushrooms, wine, tomatoes & herbs

cacciucco, spicy fish soup.

cachi, persimmons

caciatella, a creme caramel dessert

cacio, *pecorino* cheese

caciocavallo, a hard, aged cheese made of whole milk

cacio e pepe, sauce made of black pepper & *pecorino* cheese

cacio e uova, w/cheese & egg

caciotta, mild cheese

caciucco, fish soup

caffè, coffee

caffè al vetro, coffee served in a glass

caffè americano, American-style coffee (Italian coffee diluted w/hot water)

caffè con panna, coffee w/cream

alla cacciatora means in the style of the hunter

Traditionally there must be as many types of fish in the soup as c's in cacciucco.

caffè italiano.

caffè americano

caffè corretto, *espresso* w/a shot of liquor (usually brandy)
caffè doppio, coffee (a double serving)
caffè espresso, *espresso*
caffè freddo, iced coffee
caffè hag, decaffeinated coffee
caffè latte, coffee w/steamed milk
caffè lungo, coffee w/water (weaker coffee)
caffè macchiato, coffee w/a small amount of warm milk
caffè nero, black coffee
caffè ristretto, small, thick & strong coffee (stronger than an
    espresso)
calamaretto (i), small squid
calamari, squid
calamari fritte, fried squid
calamito, grey mullet
caldo (a)/caldi (e), warm or hot
caldaro, fish & potato soup
calzone (i), folded & stuffed pizza
cameriera, waitress
cameriere, waiter
camicia, in, poached
camomilla, camomile tea
camoscio, small deer (chamois)
campagnola, alla, w/vegetables & herbs
Campari, red aperitif w/a bitter, quinine taste
campo, del, wild. *Cicoria del campo* is wild chicory
candita (o), candied
canederli, dumplings made w/ham, sausage & breadcrumbs
canestrelli, sweet pastry/small snail or scallop
cannella, cinnamon
cannellini, small white beans found in Tuscany
cannelloni, large tube pasta stuffed w/fillings
cannelloni al forno, stuffed & browned in oven
cannelloni alla Barbaroux, stuffed w/ham, veal & cheese
cannelloni alla laziale, stuffed w/meat & onions
cannelloni alla napoletana, stuffed w/ham & cheese
    w/tomato & herb sauce

caffè.

calamari.

cannelloni alla piedmontese, stuffed w/veal, ham & cheese

cannocchie, see *canoce*

cannoli alla siciliana, *ricotta* cheese-filled pastry w/sugar glaze

cannolicchio, razor-shell clam

cannolo (i), custard-filled pastry w/candied fruit or sweet white cheese (*ricotta*). This also refers to a short pasta tube

canoce, Venetian word for *cannocchie* which is neither a shrimp nor a lobster but something in between similar in size to a grasshopper

cantarello, chanterelle mushroom

cantucci, almond biscuits

capellini/capelli d'angelo, thin noodle soup ("angel hair")

capelunghe, razor clams

cape sante, scallops in Venice

capitone, large eel

capocollo, smoked pork salami

caponata, cold dish of eggplant & vegetables. Eggplant, celery & onions are fried separately & cooked in a sweet & sour sauce of raisins, tomatoes, pine nuts, sugar & vinegar

caponata di melanzane, eggplant & pepper stew

cappelle di funghi, mushroom caps

cappelletti, rings of pasta filled w/ground meat. Some think it looks like a little cap

cappellini, long, thin, fine spaghetti

cappello da prete, triangular sausages ("priest's hat")

cappero (i), caper

cappesante, scallops (means "sacred shells")

capponcello ruspante al forno, roast farm-raised capon

cappone, capon

cappon magro, vegetables & fish stacked high on a plate

cappuccino, coffee w/steamed milk

capra, goat

caprese, *mozzarella* & tomatoes. *Pasta caprese* is pasta w/tomatoes, *mozzarella* & basil. *Caprese* means from the island of Capri

capretto, baby goat

capretto al forno, roasted kid stuffed w/herbs

Cantarello.

42

capretto alla pasqualina, roasted baby goat (an Easter dish)

capricciosa (o), chef's special (means "caprice" or "whim")

caprino, mild goat's cheese

caprino fresco, a fresh cheese

caprino romano, hard goat's-milk cheese

capriolo, small deer (roebuck)

caraffa, carafe

caramellato, caramelized

caramella (e), candy (not chocolate)

caramello, caramel

carbonade, beef cooked in wine & onions

carbonara, pasta w/bacon (or ham), cheese, olive oil & eggs

carbonata, grilled pork chop. Sometimes this refers to beef stew in red wine

carciofi alla giudea, deep-fried artichokes (prepared in the shape of a rose). This term means "Jewish-style artichokes"

carciofi alla romana, artichokes stuffed w/garlic, parsley & mint & cooked in olive oil & white wine

carciofi in pinzimonio, raw artichokes in an oil dressing

carciofini in umido, artichole hearts sautéed in garlic & tomatoes

carciofini sott'olio, artichokes in olive oil

carciofino (i), small artichoke

carciofo (i), artichoke. The bottoms of artichokes are the *fondi di carciofi*

cardo (i), cardoon

carmellate, caramelized

carne, meat

carne a carrargiu, spit-roasted meat

carne cruda all`albese, slices of raw steak

carne di cervo, venison

carne macinata, ground meat

carne per arrosto in pentola, pot roast

carne tritata, ground meat

carone, large white beans

carota (e), carrot

carpa/carpione, carp

carciofo.

43

carpaccio, thinly sliced raw beef w/sauce. Named by the owner of Harry's Bar in Venice after a famous Venetian painter

carpaccio di branzino, slices of raw sea bass w/a sauce

carpione, in, served cold w/vinegar sauce

carrargiu, spit-roasted

carré, sliced bread ("square")

carrè di..., roast loan of...

carrello, al, served from the food cart

carrettiera, tuna, garlic & pork sauce

carruba, carob

carta, menu

carta da musica, flat, crispy bread of Sardinia. See *pane carasau*

carteddate/cartellate, fried pastry dipped in honey

cartoccio, al, roasted (often in a paper bag, foil or other covering). The covering is opened at the table

carvi (grani di), caraway (seeds)

casa, house. *Della casa* means "house specialty"

casalinga (o), homemade

cascà, the Sardinian version of couscous

casoncelli, pasta stuffed w/ground meat

cassata, ice cream (or sweet *ricotta* cheese) w/candied fruit

cassata alla siciliana, *ricotta* cheese-filled layered cake w/sugar glaze

cassata gelata, various flavors of ice cream w/candied fruit served in wedges

casserola/casseruola, casserole

cassoela/cassoeula, pork casserole

castagna (e), chestnut

castagnaccio, chestnut cake

castagnole, chestnut fritters

castellana, stuffed veal cutlet

Castelli Romani, white table wine from the area southeast of Rome

castrato, mutton

catalogna, a type of salad green (like spinach, often cooked)

cauladda, Sardinian soup of cabbage, beans, sausage & meats

cavalla, mackerel

"Carré" means square.

Pronunciation

CA – KA
CE – CHAY
CI – CHEE
CHI – KEY
CHE – KAY

44

cavatappi, tubular pasta in the shape of a corkscrew
cavatelli/cavatieddi, homemade pasta
caviale, caviar
caviale del sud, "caviar of the south." Calabrian dish of dried
   small fish preserved in oil & powdered w/*peperoncino*
cavoletti, brussels sprouts
cavolfiore, cauliflower
cavolini di Bruxelles/cavoli di Brusselle, brussels sprouts
cavolo (i), cabbage
cavolo broccoluto, broccoli
cavolo riccio, kale
cavolo rosso, red cabbage
cavolo verde, green cabbage
cazzoeula, pork casserole
cecatelli, homemade pasta

Cavoletti.

cece (i), chickpea/garbanzo
ceche, baby eels

No thanks.

ceci alla Pisana, chickpea stew
cedrat/cedro, a large fruit that resembles a lemon.
   The peel is used for flavoring
cee alla Pisana, baby-eel dish from Pisa
cefalo, grey mullet
cena, dinner
cenci, fried pastry
Centerbe, green herb liqueur
cèpes, porcini mushroom
Cerasella, cherry liqueur
cereale, cereal
cerfoglio, chervil
cernia, grouper

EELS BREED in fresh water & mature in the sea.

Certosino, green or yellow herb liqueur.
   This is also the name for a soft & mild cheese
cervella, brains
cervo, venison
cestino di frutta, a basket of fruit

Cervella. No gracie!

cetriolino (i), pickle
cetriolo (i), cucumber

cevapcici, grilled meatballs found near Italian/Slovenian border

champagne, champagne

charlotte, sponge cake & whipped-cream dessert

Chianti, well-known medium-bodied red wine from Tuscany. *Chianti Classico* comes from the center of the Chianti region, is aged for at least one year & is more complex. *Reserva* denotes a *Chianti* aged for at least two years

chiare, egg whites

Chiaretto, young & popular rosé wine

chifferi, "c"-shaped tubular pasta

chiocciola (e), snail/sea shell-shaped pasta

chiocciolina, little snail

chiocciolini, spiral-shaped buns

chiodi di garofani, cloves

chiodino (i) a type of mushroom

chiodo di garofano, clove

ciabatta, large, course bread loaf

cialda (e), waffle/wafer

cialsons/chialzons, sweet & sour pasta

ciambella/chiambella/ciambelline, donut (not fried like North American donuts)

cibo, food

cibreo, chicken-liver dish

cicale di mare, type of shrimp (this crustacean is found off the coast of Italy. The name means "grasshopper")

ciccheti/cicheti, snacks served in Venice (similar to Spanish *tapas*)

cicina, mixture of small fried fish

cicoria, chicory/endive

ciliegia (e), cherry

cima, stuffed veal served cold

cima alla genovese, veal stuffed w/mushrooms & sausage

cimalino, *cima* served w/beans. *Cimalino di manzo* is stuffed breast of beef

cime di rape, turnip greens

cinese, Chinese

cinghiale, boar

Cinque Terre, a dry, light white wine from the spectacularly beautiful five towns on the western coast of Italy

cioccolata, chocolate

cioccolata calda, hot chocolate

cioccolato, chocolate (hot chocolate)

ciociara, a seasoned meat sauce

cioppino, fish stew (this word is usually only used in the United States)

cipolla (e), onion

cipollina (e), chive

cipolline novelle, green onions

cipollotti, spring onions

ciuppin, thick fish (& vegetable) soup

civraxin, Sardinian large bread loaf

cocco/noce di cocco, coconut

cocktail di vongole, clam cocktail (clams, olive oil & lemon)

cocktail martini, martini

cocomero, watermelon

cocozelle, zucchini

coda, tail

coda alla vaccinara, oxtail stew in a tomato & garlic sauce

coda di bue, oxtail

coda di rospo, monkfish

cognac, cognac

colazione (prima), breakfast

collo, neck

colomba, dove-shaped cake

colombacchi, wild pigeon

coltello, knife

composta, stewed fruit (compote)

composta cotta, mixed cold, cooked vegetables

con, with

conchiglie, shell-shaped pasta. *Conchigliette* is a small version used in soup

condimento (i), condiment

confetti, sugared almonds (used in weddings & special occasions)

Cinque Terre is an absolutely beautiful place.

Cocomero.

coltello.

47

confettura, jam
con ghiaccio, on the rocks
coniglio, rabbit
coniglio all'agro, rabbit stewed in red wine
coniglio all'Anconetana, a stuffed-rabbit dish
cono, cone (as in ice cream cone)
con seltz, w/soda
conserva, preserves/jam/jelly
conserva di frutta, preserves/jam/jelly
consomme, consomme (clear soup)
consomme madrilena, clear tomato soup
consomme reale, chicken consomme
contadina, alla, usually means served in a tomato
    & mushroom sauce (means "peasant woman")
conto, check/bill
contorno (i), side dish/garnish. This often refers
    to a vegetable side dish
contrafiletto/controfiletto, sirloin
copata, honey & nut wafer
coperto, cover charge
coppa, cup/goblet/small bowl.
    Coppa can also refer to smoked
    ham or smoked bacon
coppa di frutta, fruit cup/fruit cocktail
coppa di gamberetti, shrimp cocktail
coppa gelato, cup of ice cream/sundae
corda, lamb-tripe dish
cordulla, Sardinian dish madew/intestines
coregone, a type of salmon
coriandolo, coriander
cornetti, string beans
cornetto, croissant
corona, large white bean
corposo, full-bodied wine
corretto, coffee or *espresso* w/a shot of alcohol
Cortese, dry white wine
corvo, dry, light white wine from Sicily

Coniglio.
Co-NEE-LEO

Words and letters in parentheses indicate plurals.

"Cornetto" means trumpet.

cosce di rana, frogs' legs

coscetta, leg/drumstick

coscia, leg

cosciette di rane, frogs' legs

cosciotto, leg

cosciotto agnello, leg of lamb

cosciotto di porcello, leg of young lamb

costa, rib/scallop

costa di manzo, rib roast/T-bone steak

costa di sedano, celery stalk

costarelli, spareribs/pork chops

costata, chop/beef steak. *Costata di vitello* is a veal chop.
   Costata di manzo is rib steak

costata alla fiorentina, grilled beef steak

costata alla pizzaiola, braised beef steak in a tomato sauce &
   mozzarella cheese

costate, rib steak

costate d'agnello, rack of lamb

costatella, rib steak

costellata/costelleta/
   costelletine, rib steak

costicini, pork spareribs

costine, pork spareribs

costola arrostita, rib roast

costolatura, beef loin

costole di manzo, prime rib

We have found that European cuts of meat often look nothing like cuts of the same name in the States.

costoletta (e), cutlet/chop (often coated in eggs & breadcrumbs
   & fried in butter)

costoletta alla bolognese, breaded veal cutlet w/tomato sauce,
   cheese & ham

costoletta alla milanese, breaded & fried veal cutlet

costoletta alla parmigiana, cutlet breaded & baked w/
   parmesan cheese

costoletta alla siciliana, thin slices of veal or beef topped
   w/chopped garlic & *parmesan* cheese, breaded & deep-fried

costoletta alla valdostana, cutlet w/ham & cheese stuffing

costoletta alla viennese, wiener schnitzel

costoletta di vitello impanata, breaded veal cutlet

costolette di tonno, tuna steaks

costolette di vitello, veal chops

costolettine, lamb or pork chop

cotechino/coteghino, spicy pork sausage

cotognata, quince marmalade

cotogne, quince

cotoletta (e), cutlet, usually a veal cutlet

cotoletta alla bolognese, breaded veal cutlet topped w/ham, cheese & tomato sauce

cotto, cooked

cotto antico, bay leaf-flavored salami

cotto a puntino, medium done

courgette, zucchini

cozza (e), mussel

cozze alla marinara, mussels in white wine, garlic & parsley

cozze Posillipo, mussels in a spicy tomato sauce

crauti, sauerkraut

crema, cream/custard

crema caramella, custard w/caramelized-sugar topping

crema da montare, whipping cream

crema di, cream of

crema di funghi, cream of mushroom soup

crema di piselli, cream of pea soup

crema di pollo, cream of chicken soup

crema di verdura, puree of vegetables

crema fritta, fried-custard dessert

crema inglese, custard w/stewed fruit or cake

crème caramel, caramel custard

cremini, a type of mushroom

cremino, ice cream bar/a soft cheese

cren, horseradish

crescenza, a soft, buttery cheese (w/relatively low fat content)

crescionda, Umbrian dessert made from amaretto cookies, eggs, milk & unsweetened cocoa

crescione/crescione di fonte, watercress

crespelle, crêpes

ar, after-dinner drink made of artichokes

no, deer

ortar via, to go

teri di mare, mussels

tero (i), date

affeinato, decaffeinated

giorno, of the day

la casa, of the house

te, al, pasta cooked until t is still slightly firm means "to the tooth")

tice, a Mediterranean fish (dentex) similar to sea bream

ti d'elefante, tubular pasta (like *macaroni*) (means 'elephant's tooth")

of

vola/diavolicchio, usually means served w/pepper or chili peppers. Can also mean a dish cooked over a flame, since the term means "devil"

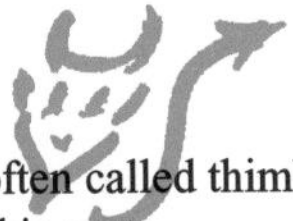

estivo, after-dinner drink

ossata, boned rib steak

stagione, in season

ali, small tubular pasta for soup, often called thimbles. *Ditalini* is the smaller version of this pasta

erso, varied

ce (i), dessert/sweet/pastry. *Dolce* can also mean sweet wine

lcetto, fruity, dry red wine from Piedmont

ci di Taglierini, sweetened noodle (taglierini) cake

cificante, artificial sweetener

rato (a), browned/golden brown

ria, alla, w/cucumbers

agoncello, tarragon

and

che, spiral pasta. Often refered to as propellers

coidali, tubular pasta w/straight edges

menthal, Swiss cheese

panata, breaded

[Handwritten margin notes:]

"Decafinato" is becoming more common but be prepared for a condescending smile.

diavolo-devil

dolce-DOL-CHAY

e means and.
é with an accent means is.

crespelle alla fiorentina, spinach crêpes

crespolino, meat-filled pancake

croccheta (e), croquette

crocchette di patate, potato croquettes

crocchette di riso, deep-fried rice balls w/cheese in the c[

crosta, crust (as in a pie crust)

crostaceo (i), shellfish

crostata, open-faced pie

crostata di frutta, fruit pie

crostini/crostoni, bread, fried or toasted in oil & topped
    w/many ingredients/croutons

crostini alla napoletana, toast w/cheese & anchovies

crostini alla provatura, toasted diced bread w/*provatura*

crostini di mare, shellfish on fried bread

crostini di milza, toast w/veal paté

crostini Fiorentina, toast w/liver paté

crostini in brodo, croutons in broth

crostone di polenta, roasted meat (usually game) served
    round base of *polenta*

crudo, raw

crusca, bran. This also refers to a bread found in Ticino w
    crust & dusted w/flour

cubbaita, nougat w/almonds, honey & sesame seeds

cucchiaio, spoon

cuccia, layered dish of slow-roasted meats, tomato sauce
    grains. A specialty in Calabria

cucina, cuisine

culaccio, rump meat

culatello, ham cured in white wine

cumino, cumin

cunillu, Sardinian word for rabbit

cuoco, chef

cuore (i), heart

cuore di sedano, celery heart

cuori di carciofi, artichoke hearts

curry, curry

cuscusu di Trapani, couscous

entrecìte/entrecote di bue, boneless rib steak

erbazzone, vegetable pie

erbe, herbs

erbette, cooked greens

espresso, *espresso* (strong, small coffee)

espresso doppio, a double serving of *espresso*

espresso macchiato, *espresso* w/a small amount of foamy milk
    on top. Compare this to *latte macchiato*

Est Est Est, a dry, semi-sweet white wine

Etna, red & white Sicilian wines

fagianella, bustard (bird)

fagiano, pheasant

fagioli al fiasco, slow-cooked Tuscan bean dish served w/garlic,
    herbs & olive oil

fagioli alla maruzzara, beans in an oregano & tomato sauce

fagioli all'Uccelloto, white beans in a tomato sauce

fagioli bianchi, white beans

fagioli bianco di Spagna, lima beans

fagioli cannellini, small white beans

fagioli con le cotiche, beans in a tomato sauce w/slices of pork

fagioli cotti al forno, baked beans

fagioli freschi, fresh beans

fagioli lessati al forno, baked boiled beans

fagioli lessi, fresh shelled beans

fagiolino (i) green bean/French bean

fagioli rampicanti, runner beans

fagioli rossi, red kidney beans

fagioli sgranati, fresh shelled beans

fagioli toscani, cooked white-bean dish

fagioli verdi, green beans

fagiolo (i), bean

fagottini, food wrapped around a filling

Falerno, dry white & red wines

fame, hungry

faraona, guinea fowl

farcito (a), stuffed

farfalle/farfallette, bow-tie or butterfly-shaped pasta

fagiolini.

fagioli.

53

farfalline (i), bow-tie or butterfly-shaped pasta

farina, flour

farinata, baked pancake made from olive oil, chickpea flour,
   salt & pepper (eaten as a snack)

farricello, barley *farricello.*

farsumagru, veal or beef roll stuffed w/ham,
   bacon, cheese, onions & parsley. A Sardinian specialty

fasolini, scallops

fatto in casa, homemade

fava (e), broad bean. Sometimes called
   fave grande or *fave España*

favarella, bean soup

favata, bean, sausage & bacon casserole

fave al Guanciale, broad beans cooked w/bacon & onions

fave e cicoria, pureéd fava beans, sautéed chicory &
   olive oil. A specialty in Apulia

fegà, liver in Venice

fegatelli di maiale, pork liver

fegato (fegatini), liver.
   Fegatini di maiale are pork livers
   Fegatini di pollo are chicken livers

fegato alla veneziana, liver & onions

fegato di vitello, calf's liver

Fernet, a bitter digestive liqueur

ferri, ai, sliced & grilled (means "on iron")

fesa, leg of veal

liver in venice, liver in Milwaukee... No gracie

fesa in gelatina, roast veal w/aspic jelly

fetta di/fetti di, slice of...

fettina, slice

fettuccine (i), long, flat, thin ribbon noodle

fettuccine Alfredo, thin ribbon noodles w/cream, butter & nutmeg

fettuccine alla Panna, thin ribbon noodles w/cream, butter &
   nutmeg

fettuccine in brodo, noodle soup

fettuna, toasted or grilled over an open fire w/garlic & olive oil

fettura di melacotogne, quince jam

fiamma, alla, flamed

fiammifero (i), match
fianco, flank
fiasco, straw-covered flask
fichi d'India/fichi indiani, prickly pears
fichi in sciroppo, figs in syrup
fichi mandorlati, figs stuffed w/almonds
fico (fichi), fig
fidelanza, spaghetti in tomato
   sauce in Liguria
filetti (di pomodoro), a sauce of sliced tomatoes
filetto (i), fillet or tenderloin
filu e ferru, Sardinian *grappa*
finferlo, an orange-colored mushroom
finocchiata, pork cured w/fennel & pepper
finocchio, fennel (some think fennel has a licorice flavor)
finocchiona, fennel-flavored salami
fiocchetto, cold cut made from the leg of pork
fiocchi, flakes
fiocchi d'avena, cereal
fiocchi di granoturco, cornflakes
fiocco, ham shoulder
fior di latte, *mozzarella* made from cow's milk
fiore, flower
fiorentina, alla, w/oil, tomatoes & herbs (sometimes w/peas or
   spinach)
fiori con ripieno, stuffed zucchini flowers
fiori di zucca, zucchini flowers served either filled w/cheese,
   battered & fried or as a pizza topping
fiori di zucca fritti, fried zucchini flowers
flambé, flamed
focaccia, flat bread topped w/olive oil & sometimes cheese
   &/or onions. Can also mean cake
focaccia barese, stuffed pizza. A specialty of Apulia
focaccia di vitello, veal patty
foglia (e), leaf
foglia di alloro/foglia di laura, bay leaf
foglia di vite, vine leaf

*fiasco.
the old
fashioned
straw-covered
bottle is
really a
novelty
now.*

foglia

55

foiolo, tripe (stomach lining)
folpetto, the Venetian word for baby octopus
fondo di carciofo, artichoke heart
fonduta, melted cheese (fondue)
fontina, mild cheese (soft & creamy)
forchetta, fork
formaggini d'Alpe, cow's-milk cheese found in Ticino
formaggini di capra, fresh goat's cheese found in Ticino
formaggio (formaggi), cheese
forno, al, baked
forte, strong
fracosta, rib steak
fragola (e), strawberry
fragole di bosco/fragoline di bosco, wild strawberries
fragolino, sea bream
fragolone, large strawberries
Frangelico, hazelnut-flavored cordial
frappé, milk shake
Frascati, dry to slightly sweet white wine
frascota di bue, rib steak
frattaglie, giblets
freddo (i)/fredda (e), cold/iced. *Tè freddo* is iced tea
fregolotta, flour, cornmeal & almond cake
fregula, dumpling soup
Freisa, dry to slightly sweet red wine
fresca (o), fresh/not cooked
freschi, wild mushrooms
fresco, al, outside (in the fresh air)
fricando, round of veal
fricassea, fricassee
fricò, cheese pancake
friggere, deep-fried (to deep fry)
frittata, omelette
frittata casalinga, plain omelette
frittata semplice, plain omelette
frittatina di patate, potato omelette
frittella (e), pancake/fritter

folpetto.

forchetta.

fragolone

Freschi –
FRESS-KEE

fritto (a)/fritti (e), fried/deep-fried
fritto alla milanese, breaded & deep-fried
fritto alla napoletana, deep-fried fish, cheese & vegetables
fritto alla romana, deep-fried sweetbreads
fritto di verdura, fried vegetables
fritto misto, mixed deep-fried fish, meat or vegetables
fritto misto alla Fiorentina, meat & vegetable fritters
frittura, frying/fry
frittura del paese, mixed floured & fried seafood
frittura di pesce, mixed dish of fried small fish, squid &
   shrimp
frizzante, semi-sparkling wine
frolla, tender (meat)/flaky pastry
frollini, biscuits
frullato, milk shake
frullato di frutta, fruit milk shake
frumento, wheat
frumentone, corn
frutta, fruit
frutta candita, candied fruit
frutta cotta, stewed fruit
frutta fresca, fresh fruit
frutta secca, dried fruit
frutti di bosco, berries
frutti di mare, seafood/seafood salad
fundador, w/brandy
funghetti, small mushroom-shaped pasta for soup
funghetto, al, sliced mushrooms cooked in garlic, onions &
   herbs
funghi trifolati, mushrooms sauteed in butter & garlic
fungo (funghi), mushroom
fuoco dell'Etna, strong, red Sicilian liquor
fusi, leg. *Fusi di pollo* is a chicken leg
fusilli, spiral-shaped pasta.
   Fusilli corti are short & *fusilli lunghi* are long
fusto, shank
galatina (in gelatina), pressed meat in aspic

frizzante.

funghi.

galantina tartufata, truffles in aspic jelly

galletta, cracker/cookie. Can also refer to a mushroom or grape

galletto, chicken (cock)

Galliano, herb liqueur (yellow in color)

gallina, chicken (hen)

gallinaccio, woodcock/chanterelle mushroom

gallina faraona, guinea fowl

gallinella, waterfowl

gallinella faraona, guinea fowl

gallo, John Dory fish in Sicily

gallo cedrone, grouse (a game bird)

gamba, leg/drumstick/shank

gamba di vitello, veal shank

gamberelli, shrimp

gamberetta di rana, frogs' legs

gamberetto (i), shrimp

gambero (i), lobster/crayfish/shrimp

gamberoni (gamberetti), large prawn

ganocchio, type of prawn

garetto, beef shank

garganelli, handmade pasta which is a square rolled into a tube

garofolato, beef stew

gaspaccio, gazpacho (the cold, tomato-based Spanish soup)

gasata/gassata, carbonated

Gattinara, full-bodied red wine

gelatina, jelly/gelatine

gelato (i), ice cream/iced dessert

gelato al tartufa, ice cream w/chocolate sauce topping

gemelli, pasta made of two strands twisted around each other. The term means "twins"

genovese, alla, w/herbs (especially basil), olive oil & garlic/w/meat & onions

germe di grano, wheat germ

germinus, almond meringue cookies from Sardinia

germogli, sprouts

gesuita, rib steak

galletto.

gamberetto.

Genovese basil is considered the most fragrant.

ghiacciato, chilled/iced

ghiaccio, ice

ghianchetti, small anchovies

ghiotta, alla, grilled or roasted

ghiozzo, mackerel

giallo d'uova, egg yolk

gianchetti, small anchovies

gianduia, chocolate & hazelnut ice cream

gianduiotti, hazelnut-and-chocolate candies

giambonette(i)/giambonetto, boned chicken roll w/filling

giardiniera, small pieces of vegetables (a garnish)

gigantoni, large tubular pasta (means "giant")

gioddu, yogurt in Sardinia

giorno, del, of the day

gin, gin ← *Good Guess!*

ginepro, juniper berry

ginestrata, chicken & sweet wine soup (a sweet & sour soup). A Tuscan specialty

girarrosto, spit-roasted

girasole, sunflower

girello, rump

glassate, glazed

gnoccata al pomodoro, tomato pizza

girasole means turns to the sun.

gnocchetti, small *gnocchi*

gnocchetti alla Sarda/gnocchetti sarda, small pasta dumplings in various sauces. A specialty in Sardinia

gnocchi, flour or potato dumplings

gnocchi alla piemontese, little balls of flour, egg & potato

gnocchi alla romana, semolina (flour) dumplings

gnocchi di patate, little balls of potato, flour & egg

gnocco fritto, deep-fried rolls of pasta

gnocco ingrassato, *focaccia* w/*prosciutto*

gnudi, means naked (w/out pasta). Stuffing only, such as in *ravioli gnudi*

gnumariddi, a sweetbread dish from Basjlicata

gomiti, "c"-shaped tubular pasta

gomma da masticare, chewing gum

gesuito means Jesuit... presumably because the priests got the best meat.

59

gorgonzola, creamy, blue cheese (best-known Italian blue)

goulasch, goulash

graffo (i), doughnut

grana, mild, hard cheese (similar to *parmesan*)

granatina, steak tartare. In most parts of Italy this term means Italian ice or shaved ice

granceola, spider crab. A specialty of Venice

granchio (di mare), crab

granciporro (i), crab

grande, large

granello, seed

gran farro, grain & bean soup

grani di, seeds of...

granita, coffee or fruit syrup served over crushed ice (a "snow cone"). Originally made from snow from Mt. Etna

grano, wheat/corn

grano duro, duram wheat

grano padano, buttery, hard, seasoned cheese w/a grainy texture

grano saraceno, buckwheat

granoturco/granturco, corn on the cob

granseola, a crab found in Venice

grappa, liquor made from grape pressings. It is extremely strong

grappolo, a bunch (as in a bunch of grapes)

grassi vegetali, vegetable oil

grasso (a), oily/fatty/fat/grease

graticola, grilled/broiled

gratin/gratinate, oven-browned w/cheese

gratinada, baked dish topped w/grated cheese & breadcrumbs

grattugiato, grated

gratuito (a), free

gremolata, minced anchovies, parsely & lemon (used as a garnish)

grenadine, veal chunks (used in casserole dishes)

griglia, alla, grilled (usually charcoal grilled)

grigliata mista, mixed grill of meats

Grignolino, high-quality red wine

Grappa can be a breathtaking experience... and that's not necessarily always good.

griglia
GREE-LEE-AH

grissino (i), long, thin bread stick

grongo, Conger eel

groppo, rump (meat)

groviera/groviera svizzera, sharp cheese w/holes (like Swiss cheese)

guancia.

guancia, pig's cheek

guanciale, al, cooked w/bacon & onions. Also refers to the delicacy of pig's cheek

guardaroba, coat room

guarnite, alla, served w/a garnish

guazzetto, usually refers to a stew (meat or fish). In Sardinia, this dish almost always contains capers

gubana, sweet bread roll (dried fruit & nut strudel found in Friuli-Venezia Giulia)

gulyas, beef stew found in Friuli-Venezia Giulia

gusti, flavors

hasce di manzo, hamburger patty

igname, yam

impanato (a), covered in breadcrumbs

impazzata di cozze/impepata di cozze, mussels cooked in their own juice w/ a black pepper, oil, parsley & garlic

incapriata, purée of fava beans & chicory

incasciata, layered dough, meat sauce, hard-boiled eggs, cheese

incluso (a), included

Indiana, all', w/curry (Indian style)

indivia, endive/chicory

indivia Belga, Belgian endive

insaccati, salami

insalata, salad

insalata all'americana, shrimp & mayonnaise salad

insalata caprese, tomatoes, basil & *mozzarella* salad. Originally a specialty on the Island of Capri, but now found everywhere in Italy

insalata cotta, cold, cooked vegetable salad

insalata di campo, field lettuce

insalata di cesare, Caesar salad

insalata di crudita, mixed raw vegetable salad

insalata cotta...
Sounds weird
but can be
great!

61

insalata di frutti di mare, seafood salad
insalata di funghi, raw mushroom salad
insalata di mare, seafood salad
insalata di patate, potato salad
insalata di petti di pollo, chicken salad w/walnuts
insalata di tonno, tuna salad
insalata di verdura cotta, boiled vegetable salad
insalata mista, mixed salad
insalata riccia, curly endive
insalata russa, diced potato & vegetable salad w/mayonnaise
insalata siciliana, salad featuring fennel & black olives
insalata verde, green salad
integrale, whole wheat
involtini al sugo, rolled veal cutlets w/ham & cheese & topped
   w/tomato sauce
involtini di cavolfiori, cabbage leaves stuffed w/meat
involtini di pesce, thin fish slices stuffed w/*prosciutto* & herbs
involtini di salvia, a deep fried sage leaf anchovy roll
involtini di vitello, veal roll usually stuffed w/salami & cheese
involtino (i), stuffed roll
iota, hearty vegetable soup (white beans, cabbage & bacon fat).
   A specialty of Trieste
Ischia, red & white wines from Southern Italy
I.V.A., abbreviation for Value Added Tax (V.A.T.)
jota, thick bean & sauerkraut soup (see Iota)
julienne, small strips of vegetables
kirsch, al, w/a clear cherry brandy
knoedel/knödeln, dumplings found in Trentino-Alto Adige region
krapfen, doughnuts (Austrian name)
laccetto, mackerel
lacerto, mackerel
Lacrima Christi, popular red,
   white & rosé wines
Lago di Caldaro, light red wine
Lagrein Rosato, rosé wine
Lambrusco, well-known red wine (sweet)
lamelle fegato, thin slices of liver sautéed in butter

There is No 'K' in the Italian Alphabet. These are German words.

Lampreda.
Non vorrei,
grazie

lampone (i), raspberry
lampreda, lamprey
lanzado, mackerel
lardarellatta alla fiama, larded & cooked on a grill
lardo, bacon/salt pork/lard
lardone, salt pork
lardoons, cured & fried pork
lardoso, meat fat
lasagne, thin layers of dough & meat, tomatoes, cheese & sauce
    (baked in the oven)
lasagne al forno, large strips of pasta cooked in sauce
lasagne alla portoghese, baked custard caramel
lasagne alla vincisgrassi, baked *lasagne* w/meatballs
lasagne verdi, spinach *lasagne*
latte, milk
latte al cacao, chocolate milk
latte di mandorla, almond milk
latte intero, whole milk
latte macchiato, steamed milk w/a small amount of *espresso*.
    Compare this to ***espresso macchiato***
latte magro, skim milk
latterini, poached fish dish
latte scremato, skim milk
latticini, small *mozzarella* balls
lattonzolo, suckling pig
lattuga (e), lettuce
lattuga romana, romaine lettuce
lauro, bay leaf
lavarello, a type of salmon
laziale, alla, w/onions
lecca-lecca, sucker/lollypop
leccia, pompano
leggero, light or weak/light wine
legume (i), vegetable
lenticchia (e), lentil
lepre, rabbit/hare
lepre in salmì, marinated rabbit ("jugged rabbit")

Latte.
generally not
drunk by
the glass.

63

leprotto, young rabbit

lessato (a), boiled

lesso, boiled. This can also refer to meat or fish stew

letterato, small tuna fish

lievito, yeast/baking powder

lievito di birra, brewer's yeast

limonata, lemonade/lemon soda

limonata.

limoncello, alcohol & lemon-zest drink

limone (i), lemon. *Al limone* means w/lemon juice

lingua, tongue. This can also refer to sole (seafood)

linguine, flat noodles

liquore (i), liqueur. *Liquore Strega* is a sweet herb liqueur

liquoroso, fortified dessert wine

liscia/lisce, refers to smooth pasta (w/out ridges)

liscio, straight. *Brodo liscio* is plain broth

lissa, pompano in Venice

lista, menu

lista dei vini, wine list

livornese, alla, usually beans in tomato sauce w/celery & onions

locale, local

lodigiano, a type of *parmesan* cheese

lomba di vitello, veal sirloin

Lombarda, alla, served fried in butter w/lemon juice & parsley

lombata, loin/leg. *Lombata di maiale* is a pork chop. *Lombata di vitello* is a grilled veal chop

lombata ai sassi, floured steak sautéed in butter w/sage & fried potatoes

lombatine, tenderloin or cut of meat for filet mignon

lombello, loin/leg

lombo di manzo, beef loin/sirloin

lonza, loin

lucanica, spicy sausage

lucerna (e), grouper

luccio, pike

lucullo, alla, raw beef (steak tartare)

Lugana, dry white wine

luganega, pork sausage. This spicy sausage from Basilicata has many similar spellings such as *luganica* & *lucanica*

lumaca (lumache), snail. *Lumache* also refers to snail-shaped pasta. *Lumachine* is a small version of this pasta used in soup

lumache alla Bourguignonne, snails w/garlic butter ("Burgundy snails")

lunga, long (as in long pasta or *pasta lunga*)

lungo, lighter *espresso*

lupo di mare, sea perch

luvasu, sea bream

maccarello, mackerel

maccarones con bottarga, Sardinian pasta w/fish eggs

maccaruni di casa, Sicilian pasta dish served w/tomato & meat sauce

maccheroni, *macaroni*

maccheroni al pettine, pasta w/ridges usually served w/ragù

macchiato, coffee or *espresso* w/milk

macco di fave, broad bean, onion & tomato soup

macedonia di frutta, fruit salad

macedonia di legumi, mixed cooked vegetables

macinata, ground. *La carne macinata* is ground beef

madera, al, cooked in Madeira wine

mafaldine, pasta ribbons

maggiorana, marjoram

magro, dish w/no meat/lean. *Ravioli di magro* is stuffed pasta w/herbs & *ricotta* cheese

maiale, pork

maionese, mayonnaise

mais, corn

malfatti di ricotta, *ricotta gnocchi*. *Malfatti* means badly made, a reference to the handmade dumplings in this dish

malloreddus, flavored dumplings found in Sardinia

malloreddus all'oristanese, saffron-flavored dumplings w/a sauce of Swiss chard, cream & eggs

maltagliata, *macaroni*

mammole, artichokes

mancia, tip

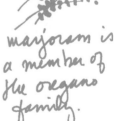

Lumaca.

marjoram is a member of the oregano family.

Mammole.

65

mandarino (i), tangerine/mandarin

mandorla (e)/mandorlata, almond

manicotti, stuffed (w/cheese & meats), baked pasta dish

mantecato, whipped ice cream. This also refers to a way to prepare cod

manzo (di bue), beef

manzo arrosto ripieno, stuffed roast *← Love it!*

manzo lesso, boiled beef

manzo salato, corned beef

manzo stufato al vino rosso, beef stewed in red wine

maraschino/marasco, w/Maraschino (cherry-flavored liqueur)

mare, di, of the sea

mare-monti, a dish served w/mushrooms & shrimp

margarina, margarine

margherita, this term is used to describe a pizza w/tomato, *mozzarella* & basil

marinara, alla, usually, but not always, means in tomato sauce (usually w/garlic & olives). The term means "of the sea" or "sailor's style", so can also refer to a dish w/seafood

marinata (o), marinated

maritozzo, soft bread roll

marmellata, marmalade/jam

marmellata d'arance, marmalade

marrone (i), chestnut. *Marrons glaces* are candied chestnuts

Marsala, fortified dessert wine from Sicily

marsala, al, in a Marsala wine (fortified dessert wine) sauce

Martini, vermouth

mascarpone, a soft, very creamy, fresh cheese (even for cheese, it is high fat)

masenette, tiny crabs eaten whole (w/the shell)/Venetian word for small crabs

matriciana, bacon, tomato & spices sauce

mattone, al, pounded flat (usually chicken) & roasted in a brick oven

mazza da tamburo, a parasol-shaped mushroom

mazzancelle/mazzancolle, very large prawns

mazzancougni, very large prawns

medaglione, medallions
medallione, a grilled ham & cheese sandwich
media, medium
mela (e), apple
melacotogna, quince
melagrana, pomegranate
melanzana (e), eggplant
melanzane al funghetto, sautéed eggplant.
melanzane alla Napoletana, eggplant Neopolitan style
   (layered w/cheese & tomato puree & baked in an oven)
melanzane alla parmigiana, eggplant *parmesan* (w/tomatoes
   & *parmesan* cheese)
melanzane ripiene, stuffed eggplant
melassa, molasses
meliga, cornmeal
melone, melon/canteloupe
menta, mint
mentine, mints
menù, menu
menù a prezzo fisso, set menu
menù turistico, fixed-price menu
merca, roast fish dish from Sardinia
merenda, late morning/afternoon snack
meringa, meringue
meringa chantilly, meringue shells filled w/whipped cream
meringato/meringhe/meringua, meringue
merlango, hake/cod/whiting
merlano, whiting, cod or hake
merluzzo, cod
messicani, veal scallops dish/veal rolls
mesticanza, mixture of salad greens
metà, half
mezzo (a), half
mezzelune ai pinoli, pine-nut cookies from Umbria
mezze maniche, short tubular pasta
miascia, bread & fruit pudding
midollo, marrow

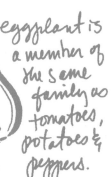

eggplant is a member of the same family as tomatoes, potatoes & peppers.

miele, honey

miglio, millet

milanese, alla, battered w/eggs & breadcrumbs & fried

Millefiori, herb-based liqueur

millefoglie, puff pastry/napoleon

millerighe, ridged tubular pasta (means "thousand lines" after the ridges in the pasta)

mimosa, sponge cake & whipped-cream dessert

minerale, mineral (as in *acqua minerale* or mineral water)

minestra (minestre), soup (usually thick soup)

minestra al farro, soup made from the grain emmer

minestra di cipolle, onion soup

minestra di fagioli, bean soup

minestra di farina tostata, toasted-flour soup

minestra di farro, "spelt" soup. Wheat (spelt) soup w/ ham bone

minestra di funghi, cream of mushroom soup

minestra di lenticchie, lentil soup

minestra di pomodoro, tomato soup

minestra di riso, rice soup

minestra in brodo, broth w/noodles or rice & chicken livers

minestra maritata, meat broth & vegetable soup

minestre di piscialetto, dandelion-greens soup

minestrina, soup (usually clear)

minestrone, bean & vegetable soup w/noodles, vegetables, rice

minestrone alla genovese, vegetable soup w/*macaroni* & spinach

minestrone verde, thick vegetable soup w/herbs & beans

mirabella (e), small plum

mirtillo (i), blueberry. The word *mirtilli* is also used for berries in general & for cranberries

mischianza, salad of wild greens, herbs & edible flowers

misoltini, salted & dried shad (fish)

misticanza, salad of wild greens, herbs & edible flowers

misto/misti, mixed

misto del golfo/misto del paese, mixed floured & fried seafood

misto mare, mixed floured & fried seafood

mitilo, mussel

moka, mocha

molto, very

montanara, alla, has many meanings but genereally means w/red wine sauce or w/ vegetables

montare, to whip (usually refers to cream)

montebianco/Mont Blanc, pyramid of sweetened chestnuts & whipped cream (named after Mont Blanc)

Montepulciano, full-bodied, dry red wine

montone, mutton

monzittas, snails in Sardinia

mora (e), blackberry

mormora, small fish found in the Mediterranean

mortadella, luncheon meat w/pistachio nuts & peppercorns

morto, pot roast

moscardino (i), small squid

Moscatello/Moscato, muscatel (table & dessert white & red wines from the muscat grape)

mostarda, mustard. This word is rarely used. Most use *senape*

mostarda di frutta, candied fruits in syrup/preserved fruits in a mustard sauce/fruit chutney

mousse al cioccolato, chocolate mousse

mozzarella, a soft, fresh (unripened), slightly sweet cheese

mozzarella di bufala, *mozzarella* made from buffalo milk

mozzarella in carrozza, fried *mozzarella* sandwich (means "in a carriage")

muddica, breadcrumbs in Sicily

muggine, grey mullet

muscoletti, shank

muscoli, mussels. This word is rarely used. Most use *cozze*

muscoli alla marinara, steamed mussels dish

musetto, salami

napoletana, ("Naples-style") w/tomato sauce (w/out meat)

nasello, whiting/hake/cod

naturale, plain/natural

nave, di, w/seafood

navone (i), turnip

`nduja, Calabrian pork sausage

Nebbiolo, full-bodied dry red wine

Navone.

69

nepitella, an herb similar to mint

nero (a), black

nervetti, calf's foot dish (tendons of calves' feet). A Venetian specialty

nespola, medlar (a tart fruit)

nidi di rondine, pasta rolls

nocciola (e), hazelnut

noccioline americane, peanuts

nocciole, nuts

noce (i), nut/walnut. Can also refer to the top round of veal

noce di cocco, coconut

nocelli, walnut-raisin cookies

noce moscata, nutmeg

nocepesca, nectarine

noci d'anacardo, cashews

Nocillo/Nocino, liquor made from walnuts

nodino (i), chop/small grilled pork chop

non, not

non fumatori, no smoking

non gassata, still or not carbonated

nonna, alla, this can be any sauce served w/pasta. The term means "grandmother" & there are as many variations of *"alla nonna"* as there are grandmothers

norcina, sausage & cheese sauce. After the town of Norcia

Norma, alla, this usually refers to a dish served w/eggplants, tomatoes, basil & sometimes *ricotta* cheese

nostrale/nostrano, home-grown/local

novellame, a spread of salted anchovies & *peperoncino* sauce

novello/novelli, fresh/tender

o, or

oca, goose

occhiate, orata (a fish)

occhi di lupo, small tubular pasta "wolves' eyes")

olio, oil/olive oil

olio d'arachide, peanut oil

olio da tavola, salad oil

nervetti... I don't think so.

non is pronounced almost like NONG.

Olio d'oliva we never leave Italy without a bottle.

olio di cartamo, safflower oil

olio di girasole, sunflower oil

olio di grano/olio di granturco, corn oil

olio di palma, palm oil

olio di semi, seed oil/corn oil

olio d'oliva, olive oil

olio santo, chili-infused oil

oliva (e), olive (*nere,* black, *verdi,* green)

olive agrodolci, olives in sugar & vinegar

olive ascolane, large green olives. *Olive all'ascolana* are olives
stuffed w/minced meat & fried in olive oil from Le Marche

ombra, glass of wine in Venice. This word is usually used at a
bar & not at a restaurant

ombrina, umbrine (seafood/bass)

omelette, omelette

omelette casalinga, plain omelette

omelette semplice, plain omelette

oranciata, orangeade

orata, a fish found in the Mediterranean (porgy)

oratino, a small *orata* fish

orecchiette, small ear-shaped pasta

orecchiette con le cime di rapa, small ear-shaped pasta
w/turnips. A specialty in Apulia

origano, oregano

ortaggi, vegetables/greens/herbs

Orvieto, light, dry, white wine from Orvieto in Umbria

orzata, almond or barley-flavored water

orzetto, barley & potato soup

orzo (i), rice-shaped pasta. Can also refer to barley

osso, bone

ossobuco (ossibuchi), braised veal shank dish. You may be
given a marrow spoon to eat the marrow in the bone

ossobuco alla milanese, veal shank, tomatoes, garlic & wine

ostrica (ostriche), oyster

ovalina, a type of *mozzarella* cheese

ovolo (i), a rare (& delicious) mushroom w/an orange & scarlet
color. Sometimes called Caesar's mushroom

pacchetto, package

paciugo, parfait

padella, in, fried

paesana, alla, usually means served w/bacon (or sausage), potatoes, carrots & other vegetables

paeta, spit-roasted turkey

pagaro/pagello, sea bream/porgy

paglia e fieno, pasta dish w/yellow (egg) & green (spinach) pasta (means "straw & hay")

pagliarino, soft, mild cheese

pagliata, a dish containing organ meat *I don't think so.*

pagnotta, loaf

pagnotta del cacciatore, game birds roasted in dough

pagro, sea bream/porgy

paiata, spit-roasted turkey

paillard, beef rib steak or veal cutlet pounded thin & grilled

pajata, a dish containing organ meat

palamito, bonito fish

palemone, prawns

pallina, scoop (as in scoop of ice cream). The word really means "marble"

palomba. They're all over the damn place.

palomba/palombaccia, pigeon

palombacci, an Umbrian dish of small birds cooked whole on a spit

palombo, dogfish/shark found in Sicily

panafittas, dried bread broken into pieces & boiled (like pasta), then served in a tomato sauce in Sardinia

panardo, a thirty-course feast served in Abruzzo

panata, bread soup

pancetta, bacon (cured pork belly)

pancetta arrotolata, rolled bacon flavored w/cloves

pan có Santi, sweet bread w/raisins, dates, honey & walnuts. "Saints' bread" is eaten around All Saints Day (November 1)

pan di Genova, almond cake

pan di Spagna, sponge cake

pandolce, cake w/dried fruit

pandoro (di Verona), star-shaped light cake w/sugar topping

72

pane, bread/loaf

pane bianco, white bread

pane bigio, whole-wheat bread

pane carasau, flat crispy bread found in Sardinia. Also known as *carta da musica* (music paper)

pane di segale, rye bread

pane e coperto, the charge for bread & for sitting at the table

pane frattau, *pane carasau* topped w/tomato sauce, grated cheese & a fried egg. A specialty in Sardinia

pane grattugiato, breadcrumbs

pane integrale, whole-wheat bread

panelle, chickpea fritters

pane nero, dark bread

pane pepato, gingerbread

pane piccante, gingerbread

pane scuro, pumpernickel bread

pane toscano, sourdough bread

pane tostato, toast

panettone, spiced cakes or coffeecakes w/candied fruits

panforte, flat, hard fruitcake

pan grattato, breadcrumbs

panicielli d'uva passula, grapes wrapped in leaves & baked

panino (i), roll/sandwich

panino imbottito, sandwich

paniscia, rice, sausage & bean soup

pan matteloch, honey bread found in the lake country

pan meino, cornmeal bread/cake (millet bread) w/elderflowers

panna, cream

panna, alla, served in a cream sauce or w/creamy gravy

panna, con, in a cream sauce/w/cream

panna cotta, rich cream custard

panna da montare/panna montata, whipped cream

pannocchia, corn on the cob

panpepato, gingerbread or hazelnut cake

pansoti/pansotti, triangular-shaped filled pasta

pan tostato, toast

panzanella, bread & vegetable salad

[handwritten note: The Italians, like the French, are fiercely proud of their bread.]

panzerotti, baked (or deep-fried) dough filled w/pork, cheese, tomatoes or other ingredients

panzoni, stuffed ravioli dish

paparot, cornmeal & spinach dish from Friuli-Venezia Giulia

pappa al pomodoro, tomato & bread soup

pappardelle, long, flat, wide pasta

pappardelle al sugo di lepre/pappardelle sulla lepre, strips of pasta w/rabbit sauce

paprica, paprika

pardulas, Sardinian pastries filled w/cream cheese

parigina, hamburger buns. In Sicily, this refers to bread

parmigiana, alla, w/*parmesan* cheese & tomatoes

parmigiana di melanzane, baked slices of eggplant layered w/*parmesan* cheese, tomatoes & *mozzarella*

parmigiano, *parmesan* cheese usually served grated

parmigiano-reggiano, the "real" name for *parmesan* cheese

partenopea, means "Naples' style", the same as **Napolitana**

Pasqualina, "Easter style" which can mean roasted in an oven w/olive oil, onion, garlic, black olives & celery. **Torta Pasqualina** is a pie featuring artichokes

passate di legumi, puree of vegetables

passatelli, pasta of *parmesan* cheese, eggs & breadcrumbs

passato, puree

passato di verdura, cream of vegetable soup

passera di mare, flounder

passera pianuzza, flounder

passerino, flounder

pasta, pasta (dough made of flour, oil, butter, eggs & water). The first course in Italy. If you find *-ette* or *-ini* after pasta, this means a smaller version of pasta. For example, *pennette* & *pennini* are smaller versions of *penne*. If you find *-oni* after pasta, this means a large pasta like *rigatoni*. *Pasta* that starts w/*taglia* is made of long, thin strips. *Pasta* can also mean pastry

pasta al forno, any pasta mixed w/a sauce & baked

pasta alla Norma, pasta w/tomatoes, basil & eggplant topped w/*ricotta* cheese

pasta asciutta, any pasta not eaten in soup
pasta con le sarde, pasta w/fresh sardines
pasta d'arachide, peanut butter
pasta di olive, olive paste
pasta e ceci, pasta & chickpea soup
pasta e fagioli, pasta & bean soup
pasta frolla, puff pastry
pasta in brodo, pasta in broth
pasta 'ncasciata, pasta baked w/eggplant, salami, tomato/basil
pasta reale (paste reali), marzipan cake (means "royal pastry")
pasta sfoglia, puff-pastry dough
paste, pastries
pastella, batter for frying
pasticceria (e), pastry
pasticcetti, small tarts
pasticciata, baked pasta (in a casserole)
pasticcini da te, teacakes/small pastries
pasticcino (i), cake/small pastry/tart
pasticcio, pastry/pie. Also the Venetian word for baked lasagne
pasticcio di maccheroni, sweet pie containing meat sauce
pastiera napoletana, *ricotta* cheese-filled pastry
pastina, small pasta usually used in soup
pastina in brodo, pasta served in soup
pastissa, pot pie
pasto, meal
patata (e), potato
patate al lesso, boiled potatoes
patate al ghiotto/patate alla ghiottona, stuffed baked potatoes
patate americane, sweet potato
patate arroste, roasted potatoes
patate bollite, boiled potatoes
patate dolci, sweet potato
patate fritte, fried potatoes/french fries
patate in padella, potatoes fried in a pan
patate lesse, boiled potatoes
patate novelle, new potatoes
patate rosolate, roasted potatoes

anti - before
pasto - meal
antipasto.

patate saltate, potatoes sliced & sautéed
patate tenere, new potatoes
patatine fritte, french fries/chips
patatine novelle, small roasted potatoes
pate/paterini, pâté
pecora, sheep/ewe
pecorino, hard, sharp cheese usually served grated. *Pecorino alla griglia* is a Sardinian specialty of grilled *pecorino* cheese
pellegrine, scallops
penne, tube-shaped pasta (cut at an angle)
pennette, smaller version of *penne*
penneziti, larger version of *penne*
pennoni, the largest version of *penne*
peoci, mussels. Also the Venetian word for "head lice"
pepata di cozze, mussels in a black pepper, oil & garlic sauce
pepato, peppered
pepe, black pepper
pepe di Giamaica, allspice
peperonata, tomatoes, peppers & onion stewed together
peperoncino (i), small, spicy pickled pepper
peperone (i), pepper
peperoni alla brace, roasted marinated peppers
peperoni imbottiti, stuffed peppers
peperoni ripieni, stuffed peppers
peperoni rossi, red peppers
peperoni sott'aceto, pickled chillies
peperoni verdi, green peppers
pera (e), pear
perciatelli, hollow spaghetti noodles
per contorno, meal includes salad or side dish
pere helene/pere elena, poached pear served in vanilla ice cream & topped w/chocolate sauce
pernice, partridge
persico, perch
pesca (pesche), peach
pesca melba, peaches in syrup w/ice cream & whipped cream
pescatora/pescatore, seafood sauce for pasta & rice dishes

pescatrice, angler fish

pesce, fish

pesce carpionata, marinated fish in herbs

pesce in saor, fish in a sauce of onion, raisin, pine nut & vinegar. A specialty in Veneto

pesce persico, perch

pesce San Pietro, John Dory fish

pesce sciabola, an eel-like fish

pesce serra, bluefish

pesce spada, swordfish

pesce stocco, cod

pesce turchino, mackerel

pesche, peaches

pesche aurora, sponge cake soaked in peach liqueur

pesto, basil, oil, garlic & pine-nut sauce

petonchio, scallops

petroniana, alla, can mean many things, most frequently means breaded & fried & topped w/melted cheese

pettine (i), small scallop

petto, breast (of poultry)

petto alla princessa, chicken floured & fried in butter & served w/an egg on top

petto all'arancio, chicken in an orange sauce

petto di pollo, chicken breast

peverada, chicken liver & anchovy sauce

pezzenta, pork salami

pezzo, piece

piacere, of your own choice (your pleasure)

piadina, soft, flat bread

pianuzza, flounder/halibut

piastra, grilled on a flat steel plate

piattino, saucer

piatto (i), dish/plate. *Piatti freddi* means cold dishes

piatto del giorno, dish of the day

piccante, highly seasoned (hot)

piccata (e), veal scallop

piccata all'allegro, veal scallop fried in butter w/lemon juice

piccata alla Lombarda, veal scallop fried in butter w/lemon juice & parsley

piccata di vitello, veal cooked in lemon & parsley

piccatina, veal scallop dish

piccioncino, young pigeon

piccione, pigeon

piccione selvatico, wild pigeon

piccolo (i)/piccola (e), small

pici, eggless pasta

piede (i), foot

piemontese, sauce w/truffles ("Piedmont style")

pietanza, dish/main course

pimento, pimento/allspice

pimiento, sweet red peppers

pinoccate/pinocchiata, almond & pine-nut cake

pinolata, pine-nut dessert cake found in Tuscany

pinolo (i), pine nut

Pinot Grigio, light, fruity white wine

pinsimonio/pinzimonio, oil, pepper & salt dressing/oil & mustard dressing for dipping

pinza, yellow flour, pine nut & raisin cake from Veneto

pipe, pasta similar to *lumache* (a snail-shaped pasta)

pisello (i), pea

pistacchi, pistachio nuts

pitta, pizza either stuffed or topped with many ingredients. Popular in Calabria

Pizza... Man's highest culinary achievent.

piviere, plover (bird)

pizza, pizza

pizza alla marinara, the "true" pizza, tomato, olive oil & oregano

pizza alla napoletana, pizza w/cheese, capers, tomatoes, anchovies, olives & *mozzarella*

pizza alla siciliana, pizza w/salami or ham, anchovies, olives, tomatoes & *mozzarella*

pizza bianca, pizza bread topped w/sea salt & olive oil

pizza capricciosa, same as *pizza quattro stagioni*

pizza di Pasqua, cheese bread

pizzaiola, w/tomato & garlic sauce

pizzaiolo, pizza man (the maker of pizzas)

pizza margherita, pizza w/tomato, basil & *mozzarella*

pizza marinara, pizza w/garlic, oil & oregano. Can also refer to a pizza w/black olives, anchovies, tomatoes & capers

pizza quattro stagioni, w/seafood, cheese, artichokes & ham in four sections. Means "four seasons" & is a pizza which has a different topping for each quarter

pizzelle, small (fried) pizzas

pizzetta, small pizza

pizzoccheri, pasta made w/buckwheat flour

polenta, cornmeal mush

polenta concia, *polenta* w/cheese

polenta di grano saraceno, buckwheat *polenta*

polenta dolce, sweet *polenta* dessert

polenta e osei, *polenta* w/roast fowl

polenta grassa, butter, fontina cheese & *polenta*

polenta pasticciata, *polenta* served w/meat sauce, cheese, mushrooms & sauce (*polenta* pie)

polipetto (i), small squid/baby octopus

polipo (i)/polpo (i), octopus

pollame, poultry

pollastra/pollastrello, young chicken

pollastrino al mattone, chicken pounded flat & roasted in a brick oven

pollo al mattone is a favorite!

polletto, spring chicken

pollo, chicken

pollo alla diavola, highly spiced, grilled chicken

pollo alla Marengo, sautéed chicken dish with many ingredients (usually tomatoes, mushrooms & onions). The dish takes its name from the town of Marengo, where Napoleon defeated the Austrians

pollo alla Romana, chicken pieces fried, bacon & garlic

pollo all'arrabbiata, "Enraged chicken" (a spicy chicken dish)

pollo arrosto, roasted chicken

pollo fritto Fiorentina, chicken marinated in oil, lemon juice & herbs

pollo in bellavista, roasted chicken dish w/vegetables

pollo novello, spring chicken

pollo piccata al Marsala, chicken pounded thin & fried in butter & Marsala wine

pollo scarpariello, boneless chicken w/lemon, garlic & parsley

polpa, meat/flesh

polpetielle, baby octopus

polpetta (e) di carne, meatball

polpetti affogati, small octopus cooked w/tomatoes (means "drowned octopuses")

polpettine (i), meatball. *Polpettine di pesce* is a seafood ball

polpettone, meat loaf

polpi arricciati, "curled octopus." An octopus dish in which the octopus is curled by beating & twirling it in a basket

polpo in purgatorio, octopus sautéed in oil w/tomatoes & peppers

pomi d'oro, the original name for tomato (means "golden apple"). It is believed that the tomato arrived in Europe w/a golden color which turned red under the hot Mediterranean sun

pommarola (salsa di), tomato sauce

pomo (i), apple

pomodoro (i), tomato

pomodoro, al, w/tomato sauce

pomodoro doppio (concentrato), thick tomato paste

pomodoro pelati, peeled tomatoes in their own juice

pomodoro pumate, sun-dried tomato

pomodoro super cirio, thick tomato pureé

pomodori con tonno, tomatoes stuffed w/tuna

pomodori secchi, sun-dried tomatoes

pompelmo, grapefruit

popone, melon

porcecellino, suckling pig

porceddu/porcheddu, Sardinian word for roast suckling pig

porcello, young pig

porchetta, roast suckling pig stuffed w/herbs

porcini, mushrooms (the wild mushroom boletus)

porco, pork

porri dorate, battered & deep-fried leeks

porro (i), leek

portacenere, ashtray

portafoglio, veal cutlet stuffed w/herbs, cheese & other ingredents. This is also the word for wallet

portata (e), course

porto, port

portoghese, usually means w/tomato sauce

porta cenere. Can't get away from it in Italy.

porzione, portion

posillipo, seafood sauce

praio, dorade (fish)/gilt-head bream

pranzo, lunch/dinner

presnitz, dessert made w/dried fruit from Fruili-Venezia Giulia

prezzemolo (i), parsley

prezzo, price

prezzo fisso, fixed price

prima colazione, breakfast

primavera, spring vegetables & cream sauce

primizie, spring vegetables or fruit

primo, first (as in *primo piatto*, first course)

principale, main (as in *piatto principale*, main course)

profiterole, filled ice-cream puff topped w/chocolate sauce & whipped cream

prosciutto, aged & cured ham

prosciutto affumicato, cured, smoked ham

prosciutto cotto, cooked or boiled ham

prosciutto crudo, salted, cured ham/Parma ham

prosciutto di cinghiale, smoked wild boar

prosciutto di San Daniele, a cured ham named after a town in the Friuli-Venezia Giulia region

prosciutto e melone, ham & melon

prosciutto di Parma, Parma ham (famous cured ham of Parma)

Prosecco, sparkling white wine from Veneto

provatura, soft, mild & sweet cheese

provenzale, onions, black olives, tomato & mushroom sauce
provolone, mild buffalo cheese
provolone dolce, mild, white, medium-hard cheese
provolone piccante, sharp cheese
prugna (e), plum
prugna secca (prugne secche), prune
pumaruolo/pumaruoro, tomato in Sicily & Campania
pumate, sun-dried tomatoes
punta di vitello, veal brisket
puntarelle, a salad green
punte di asparagi, asparagus tips
Punt e Mes, orange-flavored vermouth
    (drunk before meals)
puntino, a, medium done
punto, breast. *Punto* also means medium rare
purea, pureed/mashed
purea di fave, a puree of broad beans often spread on bread
purè di patate, mashed potatoes
puttanaio, a stew-like ratatouille (means "prostitute stew")
puttanesca, tomato, black olives, capers & garlic sauce (the
    term means "prostitute"). Allegedly named because
    prostitutes could prepare this quick meal between
    "customers"
quadrello, pork loin
quadrello d'agnello, rack of lamb
quadretti, refers to small squares of pasta
quadrucci, square-shaped pasta for soup
quaglia (e), quail
quattro formaggi, four cheeses
quattro spezie, four spices combined
    (pepper, cloves, juniper & nutmeg)
rabarbaro, rhubarb. This can also refer to an
    after-dinner liqueur
radiatori, pasta shaped like a radiator
radicchio, red endive/red chicory (bitter red lettuce)
rafano, horseradish
ragnetto, rolls

Quattro Stagione means Four Seasons

ragno, sea bass

ragno di mare, spider crab

ragù, tomato-based meat sauce

ragusano, hard, slightly sweet cheese

ramolaccio, horseradish

Rana.

ranapescatrice, angler fish

rane, frogs or frogs' legs

rannocchi, frog or frogs' legs

rapa (e), turnip

rape rosse, beet root

raspante, farm-raised (usually chicken). Means "scratching"

Ratafia, black-cherry liqueur

rattatuia, ratatouille

ravanada, horseradish sauce

ravanello (i), radish

raviggiolo, goat's-milk cheese

ravioli, squares of pasta w/stuffing. *Raviolini* are half-circle stuffed pasta

ravioli gnudi, the stuffing of ravioli (without the pasta)

ravioli verdi, spinach ravioli

razza, ray

recchie/recchietelle, the word in Apulia for *orecchiette* (ear-shaped pasta)

remolazzitt, radish

rene (i), kidney

ribes, currants

ribes neri, black currants

ribes rossi, red currants

Ribollita means Reboiled.

ribollita, vegetable soup (which means "reboiled") thickened w/bread. There are many versions of this Tuscan soup

ricciarelli, marzipan &/or almond biscuits

riccio (di mare)/ricci (di mare), sea urchin

ricciola, amberjack (fish)

riccioli, small, curly pasta

riccolo, curly endive

ricotta, similar to cottage cheese, sweetened when used in desserts

ricotta al maraschino, *ricotta* cheese w/maraschino

rigaglia (e), giblets

rigata (e), refers to ridges in pasta

rigatoni, large tube-shaped pasta (always has ridges)

rigatoni alla Norma, a Sicilian dish of pasta w/eggplant & tomato sauce

righini, bluegill

ripieno/ripiene, stuffed

riserva, mature wine

risi e bisi, creamy rice w/green peas. *Bisi* is the Venetian word for peas

Risi e Bisi... another favorite.

riso (i), rice

riso ai gamberi, rice w/shrimp

riso alla genovese, rice w/sauce of minced beef (or veal) w/vegetables

riso alla Greca, rice, vegetables & sausage dish (Greek style)

riso alla milanese, golden rice dish from Milan featuring saffron

riso alla pilota, rice w/a sausage meat sauce

riso e ceci, broth of rice & chickpeas w/tomatoes & spices

riso in bianco, white rice w/butter

riso in cagnone, boiled rice topped w/*parmesan* cheese

riso mantecado, rice cooked in butter & milk

riso nero, black rice. The rice is made black from squid ink

risoni, rice-shaped pasta for soup

risotto, creamy rice dish w/various ingredients. Served as a first course, *i primi*, after the *antipasto*

risotto ai fiori di zucca, rice dish made w/heavy cream base & zucchini flowers stirred in w/*parmesan*. A Ticino specialty

risotto alla certosina, creamy rice dish w/shrimp, mushrooms, peas & sometimes frogs' legs

risotto alla mantovana, rice dish w/salami & *parmesan* cheese

risotto alla milanese, rice w/butter, saffron, beef, zucchini & *parmesan*

risotto alla pescatora, spicy rice w/seafood

risotto alla romana, rice usually w/lamb & potatoes

risotto alla valdostana, rice w/cheese & wine

risotto alla Valenciana, the same dish as Spanish *paella*

risotto alla Veneta, rice w/mussels

risotto alla veronese, rice & ham w/mushrooms

risotto al salto, crisp rice cake

risotto di frutti di mare, rice w/shellfish

risotto di peoci, rice w/mussels

risotto nero, black *risotto.*
 Squid or cuttlefish ink makes the rice black

ristretto, reduced broth

robiola, soft, mild & slightly sweet cheese

robiolina, sheep's-milk cheese

rocciate, pastry w/fruit & nuts

rognoncini, kidneys

rognoncini al vino bianco, kidneys in white-wine sauce

rognone (i), kidney

rolatine di vitello, veal cutlets stuffed w/ham &/or cheese

rollè, roll

romagnola, usually means tomato, garlic & parsley sauce, but
 can mean many other things

romana, alla, a seasoned meat sauce w/any number of other
 ingredients

rombo, turbot

rosato, rosé

rosbif, roast beef

roscioli, red mullet in Abruzzo

rosé, rosé (blush) wine

rosmarino, rosemary

Rosolio, sweet liqueur

rospo, angler fish. *Rospo* also means toad,
 so this fish is often referred to as *pesce rospo*

rosso, red

Rosso Antico, cherry-flavored vermouth

rotella, round

rotelle/rotelline, wheel-shaped pasta

rotolo, rolled meat w/stuffing.
 Rotolo di spinaci is a spinach roll (pasta w/spinach)

rovi, blackberries

rucola, arugula

rughetta, salad green

rujolos, Sardinian sweet-cheese fritters

rum, rum

ruote di carro, pasta in the shape of a wheel (same as *rotelle*)

rustica, alla, usually means a pepper & olive sauce, but can mean many things

sagro, sea bream

salame (i), smoked sausage. *Salamino* are small salami

salame di cioccolato/ salame al cioccolato, chocolate cake in the shape of (& looks like) a salami

salamino piccante, pepperoni

salatina, greens for salad

salatini, crackers/snacks

salato, salted/salami

Salatini.

salciccia, sausage

sale, salt

salmi, in, marinated in wine, garlic & herbs (usually w/game)

salmone, salmon. *Salmoncino* is young salmon

salsa, sauce

salsa bianca, white sauce

salsa di pommarola, tomato sauce

salsa di salsiccie, sausage sauce

salsa per la cacciagione, "hunters' sauce" for cooking game

salsa tartara, tartar sauce

salsa verde, parsley-based green sauce (w/oil, lemon juice, capers & garlic)

salsicce di maiale, pork sausages

salsiccia (e), fresh sausage

saltato (i)/saltata (e), sautéed

Saltimboca means jump in the mouth

saltimbocca, veal cutlet wrapped in a layer of ham & sage

salumi, sausages

salumi cotti, cooked sausages & cured meats

salvia, sage

salvietta, napkin (paper)

Sambuca, anise-flavored liqueur. Served *con la mosca* ("w/the fly"). The "fly" is a coffee bean in the glass

sanato, young calf

sandwich, sandwich

Sangiovese, dry red wine from Emilia-Romagna

sangue, al, rare

Sanguinaccio, blood sausage (black pudding).
Also a chocolate spread made from chocolate & pigs' blood

San Pietro, John Dory fish

San Severo, dry red wine from Southern Italy

saor, sweet & sour sauce

sapa, thick sauce made from the juice of freshly pressed grapes

saporito (a), mild/tasty

sarago (saraghi), bluegill

sarda (e)/sardine, sardine

sarda, alla, tomato & meat sauce w/herbs & red wine
("Sardinian style")

sarde a beccaficu, sardines usually stuffed w/pine nuts &
raisins. A Sicilian specialty

sardella, fried baby fish minced w/olive oil & powdered
peppers from Calabria

sardina, small sardine

sardo, hard, aromatic cheese

sardoncini, little sardines

sartù, oven-baked rice dish w/tomatoes, meat balls & mushrooms

savarin, cake soaked in liquor & baked in a ring mold. The
center is filled w/fruit & whipped cream

sbrisolona, flour, cornmeal & almond cake (crumble cake)

scalogno (i), shallot

scaloppa, veal scallop (thin slices of veal)

scaloppa alla fiorentina, veal scallop w/spinach & white sauce

scaloppa milanese, breaded fried veal scallop

scaloppa napoletana, veal scallop coated in breadcrumbs

scaloppina (e), veal scallop

scaloppine alla boscaiola, veal scallop sautéed in oil & butter
& served w/an herb, black olive & onion sauce

scaloppine alla campagnola, veal scallop served in a sauce.
The term means "rustic"

scaloppine al marsala, small veal scallop in marsala wine

scaloppine al vino bianco, small veal scallop in white-wine sauce

scamorza, mild cheese (aged *mozzarella*)

scampi, shrimp/prawns

scampi all'Americana, shrimp in a tomato sauce

scanello, sirloin

scapece, fried fish in vinegar & saffron/fried vegetables which are then marinated

scarda, bream (fish)

scarola, escarole (a crispy leaf lettuce)

scarpaccia, zucchini pie (means "old shoe")

scarpena, scorpion fish

scelta, of your choice

schiacciata, flat bread (means "squashed flat")

schila, shrimp in Venice

schmarren, crêpes w/fruit & cream from Trentino-Alto-Adige

scialcione, bread loaf

sciroppato (a), cooked in syrup

sciroppo, syrup

sciroppo d'acero, maple syrup

scodella, bowl

scorfano, scorpion fish

scorfano rosso, scorpion fish

scorzonera, salsify

scotch, scotch

scodella.

scottadito, grilled lamb chops

scottiglia di cinghiale, wild-boar chops

scrippelle, omelettes cut into thin strips & served in a meat broth. A specialty in Abruzzo & Molise

sebadas, bread filled w/cheese & honey, then fried. A Sardinian specialty

secco (a), dry. *Funghi secchi* are dried mushrooms

secondo piatto, second course

sedani, the name for a small pasta similar to *rigatoni*

sedano, celery

sedano rapa, celery root

segale, rye

sella, saddle

selvaggina, game/venison

semente/semenza/senze, seeds

semi di, seeds

semi di melone, pasta noodle for soup in the shape of melon seeds

semifreddi, (half-cold) desserts frozen or refrigerated before service

semigreggio integrale, semi-whole-wheat rice

semolino, flour

semplice, plain

senape, mustard

senza, without

seppia (e), cuttlefish/squid

seppioline, small cuttlefish/squid

serpentone, pastry stuffed w/chopped figs, apples & nuts

servizio, service/service charge

servizio compreso, service included

servizio incluso, service included

servizio non compreso, service not included

servizio non incluso, service not included

sesamo, sesame

sete, thirsty

sevàdas, Sardinian deep-fried pastries

sfilatino, bread loaf

sfogie, sole

sfoglia/sfogliatella/sfogliatelli, flaky-crusted shell-shaped pastry filled w/sweetened *ricotta* cheese

sfogliata, flaky pastry

sfogliata di crema, cream puff

sformato, souffle

sfratti, sweet walnut rolls (a Christmas dessert)

sgavecio, pickled fish

sgombro (i), mackerel

sidro, cider

sigarette, cigarettes

silvano, chocolate tart

Silvestro, herb & mint liqueur

smacafam, *polenta* dish w/*asiago* cheese & sausage.

Smacafam means hunger killer

Soave, slightly dry white wine from Veneto

sodo/sode, hard boiled

soffritto, sautéed/stock (the base for soup or the sauce for pasta) often made w/pigs' organs. Can also refer to slightly fried or browned onions

sogliola, sole   *Sogliola* SO-LEE-OH-LA

sogliola all'Arlecchino, sole served w/a cream sauce

sogliola alla mugnaia, sole sautéed w/lemon, butter & parsley

sogliola margherita, sole covered w/Hollandaise sauce

soia, soy

sopa, soup

sopa cauda, soup w/bread & roast pigeon

soppressa, sausage

soppressata, sausage/sausage made from pig's head

sorbetto, sherbet/sorbet

sorbetto al calvados, sherbet-flavored w/apple brandy

sorrentina, often refers to a tomato, basil & mozzarrella sauce

sottaceti, pickles

sottaceto, pickled

sottoaceti, pickled vegetables/pickles

sottofiletto, beef or veal loin

sott'olio, in olive oil

sottonoce, top round of veal

spaccatina, bread loaf

spaghetti, spaghetti (long, thin pasta)

spaghetti aglio e olio, spaghetti w/olive oil & garlic

spaghetti alla bolognese, spaghetti w/meat sauce

spaghetti alla carbonara, spaghetti w/cream, bacon, cheese, egg

spaghetti alla checca, spaghetti w/raw tomatoes, basil & garlic

spaghetti alla gricia, spaghetti w/onions, bacon, pepper & grated cheese

spaghetti all'amatriciana, w/tomato sauce, cheese & garlic

spaghetti alle vongole, spaghetti w/clam sauce

spaghetti al ragù, pasta w/meat & tomato sauce

spaghettini, thin spaghetti

spaghetti pomodoro e basilico, spaghetti w/tomatoes & basil

spalla, shoulder

spanocci, very large prawns

sparaci, asparagus in Venice

sparnocci, type of shrimp

specialità della casa, specialty of the house

specialità di questa regione, specialty of the region

specialità di questo ristorante, specialty of the restaurant

specialità locali, local specialties

specialità regionali, regional specialties/local dishes

speck, cured ham found in the Trentino-Alto Adige region

spelt, a hard wheat

speziato, spicy

spezie, spice

spezzatino, meat or poultry stew/little pieces

spezzato, a stew

spicchio (d'aglio), clove (of garlic)

spiedini alla corsara flambe, grilled meat served "flaming"

spiedino (i), any dish roasted on a skewer

spiedino di mare, pieces of grilled fish on a skewer

spiedo, allo, on a spit

spiga di grano, ear of corn

spigola, sea bass/grouper

spinaci, spinach

spiza di grano, ear of corn

spremuta, fresh fruit drink

spugnola, morel mushroom

spumante, sparkling wine

spumone (i), ice cream w/candied fruit, nuts & whipped cream

spumoni al croccante, *spumoni* topped w/toasted, caramelized
  almonds

spuntatura, breast of...

spuntino, snack

stagionato (a), well aged

stagione (i), season (in season)

starna, a type of partridge

stecca di, bar of

stecchi fritti, fried kebabs

stecchino, toothpick/skewer

stellette/stelline, star-shaped pasta

stinchetti, marzipan cakes (in the shape of human bones)

stinco, braised veal or pork shank. The most common version of this dish is ***stinco di maiale al forno***, a whole pork shank oven-roasted w/wine, garlic & rosemary

Stinco actually means shin bone.

stoccafisso, dried cod

storione, sturgeon

stracchino, a soft, creamy white cheese

stracciate, scrambled eggs

stracciatella, egg-drop soup. This can also refer to chocolate-chip ice cream

stracotto, beef stew w/pork sausage/pot roast

strangolapreti, see *strozzapreti*

strangozze, see *stringozzi*

strapazzate, scrambled

strascinati, shell-shaped pasta

stravecchio, *parmesan* cheese aged at least three years

Strega, a strong herb liqueur

strigghie, red mullet in Sicily

stringozzi, a homemade pasta from Umbria

strisce, ribbon noodles

strozzapreti, dumplings or *gnocchi* w/meat sauce.

strudel, this famous pastry roll can be found in Trentino-Alto Adige

Strozzapreti means Priest stranglers. A gluttonous priest supposedly choked to death on one.

strutto, lard

stufatino, pot roast or stew

stufato, braised/stewed/stew

stuzzicadenti, toothpicks

stuzzichino (i), appetizer

succhi di frutta, sweetened fruit juice

succo, juice

succo di frutta, fruit juice

succu tunnu, dumpling soup

Succu tunnu. Never had it but love the name.

sufflé, soufflé

sugna, lard

sugna piccante, a spicy sauce made from pork fat (added to dishes in Basilicata)

sugo, sauce/gravy/juice

sugo, al, w/tomato sauce

suino, pork

suppli/suppli di riso, breaded & deep-fried rice balls usually filled w/ham & cheese

suprema di pollo in gelatina, chicken breast in aspic

suro, mackerel

susina (e), plum

tacchino, turkey *tacchino*
TA-KEE-NO

tagliata di manzo, grilled beef

tagliatelle, short ribbon noodles

taglierini, thin noodles

taglierini alla chitarra, a pasta dish featuring a sheet of pasta cut w/a cutter called a *"chitarra"* or guitar

tagliolini, very narrow, thin flat noodles

tajarin, egg noodles found in Piedmont & Valle d'Aosta

taleggio, cheese w/a mild, soft, buttery flavor

taralli, biscuits made in the shape of a ring

tartara, alla, raw w/lemon sauce

tartaruga, turtle

tartina (e), open-faced sandwich/tart.
  Tartine are often appetizers

tartufi di cioccolato, chocolate "truffles" (chocolate-coated ice cream)

tartufi di mare, small clams/cockles

tartufo (i), truffle (funghi that grows around tree trunks)

tartufo di gelato, ice cream w/chocolate sauce topping

tartufo nero, black truffle from Tuscany

tasse, taxes. Menus will often indicate if *tasse e servizio* (taxes & service) are included

tavola (o), table

tavola calda, snack bar/fast food

tavoletta di cioccolata, chocolate bar

di té.

tazza, cup

tè, tea

tè cinese, China tea

tè d'India, Indian tea

tè freddo, iced tea

tegamaccio, lake-fish stew from Umbria

tegame/tegamino, al, sautéed

teglia, alla, pan-fried.

teglia di pesce spada, marinated swordfish dish

tellina (e), clam

teneroni, veal chops

terrina, tureen

testa, head. *Testa di vitello* is calf's head

testina, head

testuggine, turtle

tiedde, fish casserole from Apulia

tiella, any dish with baked layers of ingredients

tiella di agnello, roasted lamb dish

tiella di riso e cozze, mussels, rice & potato dish found in Apulia

tigelle, flat bread

timbale/timballo, meat & vegetable casserole w/layers of pasta

timo, thyme

tinca (tinche), tench (seafood)

tiramisù, sponge cake soaked in *espresso* & brandy w/cream & chocolate. *Marsala* can also be used in this delicious dessert

tirolese, alla, usually means w/fried onion rings

Tiramisu made its way to Italy from the U.S.

tisana, herbal tea

tisana al cinorrode, rose-hip tea

tisana al tiglio, lime tea

tisana camomilla, camomile tea

tocco di funghi, mushroom sauce

toc de purcit, pork stew w/white wine from Friuli-Venezia Giulia

toma, sharp cheese

tomini, fresh cheese from Piedmont

tonarelli/tonarrelli/tonnarelli, thin string pasta

tondino, bread loaf

tonica, tonic water

tonnato, in a tuna sauce. Can also refer to a cold veal dish

tonnetto, small tuna

tonno, tuna

topinambur, artichoke
(Jerusalem artichoke)

tordo (i), thrush (a bird)

torlo, yolk

torrone, nougat

Torrone is immensely popular in Italy!

torta (e), tort/cake/pie

torta al pesto, spinach & cheese pie/flat
bread cooked over hot stones in Umbria
& filled w/cheese, meat or greens

torta di frutta, fruit tart

torta di gelato, ice-cream cake

torta di mele, apple tart

torta di tagliatelle, egg-noodle cake

torta di verdure, sweet vegetable pie
(similar to American pumpkin pie)

torta giandiua, chocolate & nut cake

torta meringa, large meringue pie filled w/fruit & topped
w/whipped cream

torta millefoglie, napoleon (layers of pastry filled w/ice cream
or whipped cream & topped w/frosting)

torta Pasqualina, Easter puff-pastry cake

torta rustica, cornmeal-cake dessert

torta sbrisolona, flour, cornmeal & almond cake (crumble
cake)

torta tarantina, potato pie *← Love it!*

torta turchesca, rice-pudding tart
from Venice

torta zuccotto, liquor-soaked sponge cake
filled w/ice cream or whipped cream,
chocolate & candied fruits

tortelli di zucca, pasta stuffed w/pumpkin

tortellini, filled pasta rings
tortello (i), small doughnut/fritter
tortellone (i), a larger *tortellini* pasta
tortiera, cake/pie
tortiglione, almond cakes
tortiglioni, tube-shaped pasta (larger than *cannelloni*)
tortina di marmellata, jam tart
tortini di riso, rice cakes
tortino, tart/cheese & vegetable tart similar to quiche
tortino di carciofi, fried-artichokes-and-egg dish
toscana, alla, w/tomatoes & herbs
tostato (a), toasted
totano (i), squid
tournedos, small tenderloin steaks
tovaglia, table cloth
tovagliolo, napkin
tozzetti, hazelnut & almond biscuits (w/an anise flavor)
tracina dragone, a fish named "dragon" after its dangerous spines
tramezzino, small sandwich
trancia/trancio, piece/slice
trattaliu, cooked lamb intestines. A specialty in Sardinia
trenette, long, flat, thin ribbon noodles
trifolati, sliced mushrooms cooked in butter, garlic & oil
trifolato, w/truffles
triglia (e), red mullet
triglia alla Livornese, red mullet cooked w/tomatoes, garlic & parsley
trigoli, water chestnuts
trippa (e), tripe
trippa alla fiorentina, braised tripe & minced beef w/tomato sauce & cheese
trippa alla milanese, tripe w/onions, carrots, tomatoes, beans & leeks

My Italian teacher from Chioggia makes the best tortellini in the world.

Tovagliolo
TOV-A-LEE-OH-LO

You can put all the "ALLA"s you want on trippa and it's still TRIPE.

trippa alla romana, tripe in a tomato & vegetable sauce
tritato (a), ground (as in ground beef)
trofie, pasta similar to *gnocchi*
trombetta da morto, a type of mushroom
trota (e), trout
trota alle mandorle, stuffed-trout dish
trota di ruscello, river trout
trota iridea, rainbow trout
trota salmonata, salmon trout
trota spaccata, trout split in two, dipped in batter & deep-fried
trotella, trout
tuaca, a mixture of brandy, citrus fruits & herbs
tubetti, *macaroni*
tubi, refers to all tubular pasta
tuorlo, yolk
tutto compreso, all included
ua, grapes in Venice
ubriaco, cooked in red wine
uccelletti/uccelli, small birds (of all kinds) usually spit-roasted
uccelletto, all', w/tomato sauce & sage. *Piselli all' uccelleto* is
   peas cooked in tomato sauce w/sage
uccelli scappati, pork, pork sausage &/or small-bird kebabs
ueta, raisin in Venice
uliva, olive
umido, in, stewed
uopa, sea bream
uova, eggs
uova affogate, poached eggs
uova affogate nel vino, eggs poached in wine 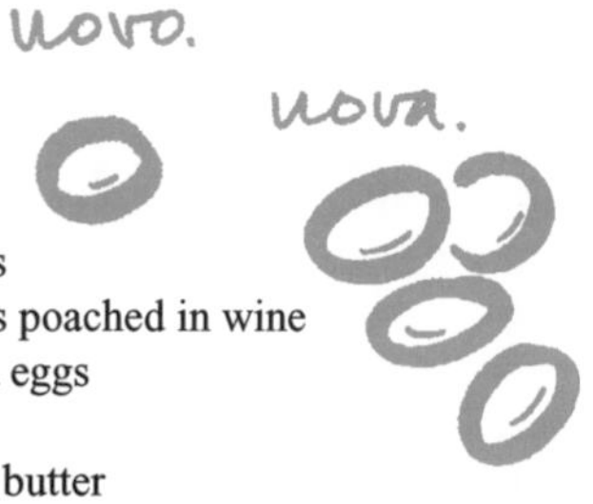
uova à la coque, soft-boiled eggs
uova albume, egg whites
uova al burro, eggs fried in butter
uova al guscio, soft-boiled eggs
uova alla campagnola, eggs w/diced vegetables & cheese
uova alla coque, boiled eggs
uova alla fiorentina, fried eggs served on spinach
uova all'americana, fried eggs (usually served w/bacon)

Handwritten margin notes:
Trombetta da morto... This sounds ominous.
Tubi or not tubi...
uovo.
uova.

uova alla russa, similar to deviled eggs
uova all'occhio di bue, fried eggs
uova al tegame con formaggio, fried eggs w/cheese
uova barrotte, soft-boiled eggs
uova bollite, soft-boiled eggs
uova frittata/uova fritte, fried omelette
uova frittata al pomodoro, tomato omelette
uova frittata al prosciutto, ham omelette
uova in camicia, poached eggs
uova molli/uova mollette, soft-boiled eggs
uova ripiene, stuffed eggs
uova semplice, plain omelette
uova sode agli spinaci, eggs florentine
uova tonnate, hard-boiled eggs in tuna sauce
uovo (a), egg
uovo fritto (uova fritte), fried egg
uovo sodo (uova sode), hard-boiled egg
uovo strapazzatto (uova strapazzate), scrambled egg
uva, grapes
uva bianca, green grapes
uva nera, black grapes
uva passa/uva passita, raisins
uva secca, raisin
uva spina, gooseberry
uvetta, white raisins
vaniglia, vanilla
valdostana, alla, usually means served w/ham & cheese (means "Valle d'Aosta style")
valigetta, roasted veal breast
Valpolicella, light (slightly bitter) red wine from Veneto
vapore, a, steamed
vario/vari, assorted
Vecchia Romagna, wine-distilled brandy
vegetable, vegetable
vegetariano (a), vegetarian
velluta, creamy soup
veneziana, alla, w/onions, white wine & sometimes mint

ventaglio, scallop

ventresca, white-meat tuna. Can also mean a boiled pork dish

verde, green/green pasta (w/a spinach base)

verde in pinzimonio, vegetable dip

Verdicchio, a dry white wine from Le Marche

verdura (e), green vegetable

verdure cotte, cooked vegetables

vermicelli, small spaghetti noodles

vermut, vermouth (popular vermouths include "Cinzano" or "Martini")

verza, cabbage

verzelata, grey mullet

i vini.

vincigrassi/vincisgrassi, baked lasagna dish

vincotto, a spread made from grapes

vinello, light wine

vino (i), wine

vino amabile, sweet wine

vino asciutto, very dry wine

vino bianco, white wine

vino brut, very dry wine

vino corposo, full-bodied wine

vino da tavola, table wine
(the lowest-quality wine made
from any combination of grapes)

vino del paese, local wine

vino de pasto, table wine

vino dolce, sweet wine

vino frizzante, sparkling wine

vino leggero, light wine

vino nostrano, local wine

vino novello, new wine

vino rosatello, rosé wine

vino rosato, rosé wine

vino rosé, rosé (blush) wine

vino roseo, rosé wine

vino rosso, red wine

*vino di tavola
is low quality
wine but not
necessarily bad.*

Vin Santo/Vinsanto, dessert wine from Tuscany & Trentino

99

vino secco, dry wine

vino semi secco, semi-sweet wine

vino spumante, sparkling wine

vino tipico, local wine

violino, cured leg of goat

visciola, wild cherry

vitellini, very young veal

vitello, veal

vitello all'uccelletto, diced veal & sage simmered in wine

vitello tonnato, cold veal w/tuna sauce

vodka, vodka

vol-au-vents, filled pastry shells

vongola (e), small clam

vongole, alle, in a clam sauce

vongole oreganate, clams baked or broiled w/oregano

whisky, whiskey

wurstel, hot dogs (similar to smoked hot dogs)

yogurt/yoghurt, yogurt

yogurt magro, low calorie yogurt. *Yogurt intero* is not low fat

zabaglione/zabaione, custard dessert flavored w/Marsala

zafferano, saffron

zalettini, shortbread cookies from Venice

zampa (e), pig's (or beef) feet

zampetto, pork leg

zampone, spicy sausage shaped like a pig's foot

zampone di maiale, stuffed pigs' feet

zelten, dried fruit & nut cake from Trentino-Alto Adige

zenzero, ginger

zèppola, doughnut/fritter

zesti, orange or lemon peel (can also be candied)

ziba, fragrant herb from Sardinia

zimini, in, cooked w/vegetables. *In zimino* can refer to spinach or Swiss chard stewed w/cod or squid & tomatoes

zimino, Sardinian fish stew

zingara, alla, "Gypsy style." Each chef has his or her own version of this sauce of many ingredients

zite (i), narrow, hollow-tube pasta

zucca, pumpkin or squash
zucca ovifera, squash
zucchero, sugar
zucchero al velo, powdered sugar
zucchero a zollette, lump sugar
zucchero greggio, brown sugar
zucchero grezzo, brown sugar
zucchero in pezzi, lump sugar
zucchero in polvere, powdered sugar
zucchine al burro versato, zucchini w/black-butter sauce
zucchine farcite, zucchini filled cheese, ham & mushrooms
zucchine fritte, deep-fried strips of zucchini
zucchine scapecce, pieces of zucchini fried in oil w/garlic
zucchine trifolate, sliced zucchini in butter, parsley & garlic
zucchino (i), zucchini
zucchio, zucchini
zuccotto, ice cream-filled cake
zuchette, zucchini
zuppa, soup
zuppa alla coltivatore, vegetable soup with diced bacon
zuppa alla pavese, soup w/croutons, grated cheese & poached egg
zuppa di cipolle alla Francese, french onion soup
zuppa di cozze, mussel soup
zuppa di datteri, fish-soup specialty of Liguria
zuppa di farro, spelt & bean soup   *Zuppa di Farro...*
zuppa di frutti di mare, seafood soup   *love it.*
zuppa di pesce, fish stew
zuppa di pollo, chicken soup
zuppa di telline, soup w/tiny clams
zuppa di verdura, vegetable soup
zuppa di vongole, clam soup w/white wine
zuppa d'orzo, barley & potato soup
zuppa fredda, cold soup
zuppa inglese, not a soup at all. Sponge cake soaked in liquor
    w/cream filling & whipped cream
zuppa pavese, clear soup w/a poached egg
zuppa valdostana, cabbage soup from the Val d'Aosta region

Restaurants

Listed below are restaurants
known for serving regional
specialties. Phone numbers
and days closed often change,
so it's advisable to check
ahead. The telephone country
code for Italy is 39. Prices are
per person and without wine.
Credit cards accepted unless
noted.

Inexpensive: under $10
Moderate: $10-20
Expensive: over $20

Alberobello

Trullo d'Oro
27 Via F. Cavallotti
080/4321820
Closed Mon. and Jan.
Unique restaurant in *trulli*
(limestone igloo-shaped hous-
es) serving the cuisine of
Apulia.
Moderate

Amalfi

Da Gemma
10 Salita Fra' Gerardo Sasso
089/871345
Closed Wed. and Jan.
Specialties of Campania
(especially seafood) with
summer dining on the terrace.
Moderate-expensive

We think, hope and pray that our restaurant list is current & correct, but remember... things change. Call first or do a "walk by" in the afternoon. Stop in, make a reservation— they'll love you for it.

Aosta

Piemonte
13 Via Porta Pretoria
0165/40111
Closed Sun.
Valdostan cuisine served
inside the Roman walls.
Moderate

Ascoli Piceno
Ristorante Tornasacco
36 Piazza del Popolo
0736/254151
Closed Fri. and part of July.
Taste the specialties of Le
Marche at this family-run
restaurant.
Moderate

Assisi
Hotel Subasio (Ristorante)
2 Via Frate Elia
075/812206
Umbrian specialties in the
shadow of the Basilica of St.
Francis and with the best view
in town from the dining terrace.
Moderate

Bergamo
Taverna del Colleoni
dell'Angelo
7 Piazza Vecchia
035/232596
Closed Mon. and part of Aug.
The specialties of Lombardy
and the Lake District served
in historic building.
Moderate-expensive

Bolzano
Zur Kaiserkron
1 Piazza Della Mostra
0471/970770
Closed Sat. (dinner) and Sun.
Local dishes of Trentino-Alto
Adige, in historic building.
Moderate

Cagliari
Dal Corsaro
28 Viale Regina Margherita
070/664318
Closed Sun. and Aug.
Lively restaurant serving
Sardinian specialties.
Moderate-expensive

Capri
Da Gemma
6 Via Madre Serafina
081/8377113
Closed Mon.
Restaurant-pizzeria serving
Caprese specialties (especially
seafood).
Moderate

Florence
Benvenuto
Corner Via Mosca & Via Neri
055/214833
Closed Sun.
Small *trattoria* serving
Florentine specialties and a
favorite of budget travelers.
Inexpensive

Buca dell'Orafo
28R Volta dei Girolami
055/213619
Closed. Sun., Mon. and part
of Aug. No credit cards.
Tuscan specialties served in
the cellar of a former gold-
smith shop (*orafo*) near the
Uffizi.
Inexpensive-moderate

Cantinetta Antinori
3 Piazza Antinori
055/292234
Closed weekends and Aug.
Tuscan cuisine served in a
palazzo and known for its
wine list.
Moderate

Il Cibreo
118R Via dei Macci (near Via
di San Giuseppe)
055/2341100
Closed Sun., Mon. and Aug.
Florentine cuisine at this
attractive and popular restaurant, café and trattoria.
Moderate (in the trattoria)-
expensive (restaurant)

Trattoria Le Mossacce
55R Via del Pronconsolo
(near Piazza del Duomo)
055/2943611
Closed Sun. & Aug.
Share a table with locals and
dine on Florentine cuisine at
reasonable prices. We'll for-
give them for the English
menus.
Inexpensive-moderate

Vivoli
7R Via Isola delle Stinche
055/292334
Closed Mon. and Aug.
The best ice cream shop
(*gelateria*) in Italy.
Inexpensive

Genoa
Gran Gotto
69R Viale Brigata Bisagno
010/564344
Closed Sun. and Aug.
Ligurian specialties in elegant
setting (jacket and tie
required).
Expensive

L'Aquila
Tre Marie
3 Via Tre Marie
0862/410109
Closed Mon. and Aug.
Local specialties of Abruzzo
& Molise in the capital of
Abruzzo.
Moderate-expensive

Lumaca.

Lugano, Switzerland
La Tinera
2 Via dei Gocini
091/9235219
Closed Sun. and Aug.
Small tavern serving Ticino
specialties.
Inexpensive-moderate

Lerici
Conchiglia
2 Via Mazzini
0187/967334
Closed Wed.
Seafront restaurant specializing in fresh seafood.
Moderate

Mantua (Mantova)
L'Aquila Nigra
4 Vicolo Bonacolsi
0376/327180
Closed Sun., Mon. and Aug.
Elegant dining (featuring the cuisine of Lombardy) in a
15th century *palazzo*.
Moderate-expensive

Maratea
Taverna Rovita
13 Via Rovita
0973/876588
Closed Tue. and winter.
Country restaurant serving
Basilicata cuisine.
Moderate-expensive

Milan
Bagutta
14 Via Bagutta
02/76002767
Closed Sun. and Dec. 24 -
Jan. 6
Popular *trattoria* serving specialties of Lombardy.
Moderate-expensive

Boeucc
2 Piazza Belgioioso
02/76020224
Closed Sat. and Aug.
Milan's oldest restaurant serving Milanese food in an elegant setting near the Duomo.
Moderate-expensive

Peck
4 Via Victor Hugo
02/876774 (restaurant)
Closed Sun. and part of July
Restaurant, delicatessen, cafeteria, take-out counter and
wine bar all at this gourmet
food store.
Expensive (restaurant) - moderate-inexpensive (cafeteria)

Savini
Galleria Vittorio Emanuele II
02/72003433
Closed Sun. and part of Aug.
The best of Lombardy served
in the Galleria.
Expensive

Monterosso

Il Gigante
9 Via IV Novembre
(Monterosso al Mare)
0187/817401
Closed Tue.
Ligurian seafood served in
this charming Cinque Terre
town.
Moderate

Orta San Giulio

Olina
40 Via Olina
0322/905656
Regional specialties at reasonable prices in this picturesque
town on Lake Orta.
Moderate

Orvieto

Le Grotte del Funaro
41 Via Ripa Serancia
0763/343276
Closed Mon.
Umbrian specialties served in
caves beneath Orvieto.
Moderate

Palermo

Charleston
30 Piazza Ungheria
091/321366
Closed Sun. The restaurant
operates in the summer
months at Mondello (north of
Palermo) at Viale Regina

Elena 091/450171.
Sicilian specialties served in
elegant restaurant.
Moderate-expensive

Perugia

Il Falchetto
20 Via Bartolo
075/5731775
Closed Mon.
Umbrian specialties in
medieval dining rooms.
Moderate-expensive

Pisa

Bruno
12 Via Luigi Bianchi
050/560818
Closed Mon. (dinner) and
Tues.
Classic Tuscan food near the
leaning tower.
Moderate

Portofino

Il Pitosforo
9 Molo Umberto I
0185/269020
Closed Tues, and Jan.
Famous and expensive, this
harbor-side restaurant serves
Ligurian specialties.
Expensive

farfalle.

Positano

Buca di Bacco
8 Via Rampa Teglia
089/875699
Closed Nov. - March
Specialties of Campania at
this seaside restaurant/café.
Moderate

Ravenna

Tre Spade
136 Via Faentina
0544/500522
Closed Mon. and Aug.
Housed in an old mill, this
restaurant serves the food of
Emilia-Romagna.
Moderate

Reggio di Calabria

Villeggianti
31 Via Eremo-Condera
0965/25021
Closed Sun.
Unpretensious restaurant
serving Calabrian specialties.
Inexpensive-moderate

Rome

Antico Arco
7 Piazzale Aurelio
06/5815274
Closed Mon.
Fine Roman food and wine at
reasonable prices at the top of
Janiculum Hill.
Moderate

Bacaro
27 Via degli Spagnoli
06/6864110
Closed Sun.
Small, unpretentious restaurant. It's hard to *Just ask*
find and near *Jeanne &*
the Piazza *Jerry.*
Montecitorio.
Moderate

Bolognese
Piazza del Popolo
06/3611426
Closed Mon. and part of Aug.
Bolognese cuisine served near
the Piazza del Popolo.
Moderate

La Campana
18 Vicolo della Campana
06/6867820
Closed Mon.
Simple Roman fare near the
intersection of Via Font. Bor-
ghese and Via della Scrofa.
Moderate

La Carbonara
23 Piazza Campo dei Fiori
06/6864783
Closed Tue. and part of Aug.
Trattoria serving Roman cuisine including *carbonara*
(hence the restaurant name).
On Piazza Campo dei Fiori.
Moderate

Castroni
196 Via Cola di Rienzo
06/6874383
A food market where you can buy specialties from every region of Italy.
Inexpensive

La Cisterna
13 Via della Cisterna
06/5812543
Closed Sun.
Regional favorites of Lazio served in family-run restaurant in Trastevere (near the Tiber River).
Moderate

Enoteca Corsi
89 Via del Gesú
06/6790821
Closed Sun. (Aug. Lunch only)
A few blocks from Piazza Rotonda, this affordable wine tavern serves Roman cuisine.
Inexpensive

Romolo
8 Via di Porta Settimiana
06/5818284
Closed Mon. and Aug.
Strolling musicians and Roman cuisine in this historic restaurant located in Trastevere.
Moderate

Rosetta
8 Via della Rosetta
06/6861002
Closed Sun. and part of Aug.
Located near Piazza della Rotonda and known for its (very expensive) seafood.
There is no meat on the menu.
Expensive

Sabatini
13 Piazza Santa Maria
06/5812026
Closed part of Aug.
Lively and popular restaurant in Trastevere serving Roman cuisine (especially seafood).
Expensive

La Terrazza
49 Via Ludovisi
06/478121
This very expensive restaurant in the Hotel Eden (several blocks off the Via Veneto) offers great food with a view of St. Peter's.
Expensive

Aglio.

Vecchia Roma
18 Piazza Campitelli
06/6864604
Closed Wed. and part of Aug.
No credit cards.
A great place to dine outdoors
in the summer months, this
trattoria serves classic Roman
fare in the Jewish Ghetto.
Moderate

San Gimignano

Bel Soggiorno
91 Via San Giovanni
0577/940375
Closed Wed.
Tuscan specialties served in a
100-year-old hotel located in
this beautiful walled town.
Moderate

Siena

Le Logge
33 Via del Porrione
0577/48013
Closed Sun.
Tuscan dishes at *trattoria* near
the Piazza del Campo.
Moderate

Enoteca Italica
Fortezza Medicea/Viale
Maccari
0577/288497
Taste wines from every region
of Italy.
Inexpensive-moderate

ANITRA.

Taormina

Luraleo
27 Bagnoli Croce
0942/24279
Closed some Wed.
Indoor and outdoor dining
specializing in Sicilian dishes.
Moderate

Trieste (San Giovanni)

Suban
2 Via Emilio Comici
040/54368
Closed Tue. and part of Aug.
In the hills two miles north of
Trieste, this *trattoria* serves
regional specialties of Friuli-
Venezia Giulia.
Moderate

Turin

Vecchia Lanterna
21 Corso Re Umberto
011/537047
Closed Sun. and part of Aug.
Historic restaurant specializ-
ing in the cuisine of
Piedmont.
Expensive

Venice

Da Arturo
3656 Calle degli Assassini.
Located between Campo S.
Angelo and Campo Manin.
041/5286974
Closed Sun. and Aug. No
credit cards.
No seafood at this tiny, popu-
lar restaurant.
Moderate-expensive

Al Covo
3968 Campiello della
Pescaria.
Arsenale vaporetto. Located
off of Riva degli Schiavoni.
041/5223812
Closed Wed. and Thurs. No
credit cards.
Fresh Venetian specialties
(especially seafood) at this
small *osteria*.
Expensive

Da Ivo
1809 Calle dei Fuseri.
San Marco vaporetto. Located
near Campo S. Luca.
041/5285004
Closed Sun., Mon. and Jan.
Comfortable restaurant serving Venetian (and Tuscan)
specialties.
Expensive

Harry's Bar
1323 Calle Vallaresso.
San Marco vaporetto.
041/5285777
Closed Mon.
Famous restaurant serving
Venetian specialties. The food
is very expensive, so you may
just want to have a martini or
a *Bellini* (peach juice and
Prosecco) at the bar.
Expensive

Taverna La Fenice
1939 Campiello de la Fenice
San Marco vaporetto.
041/5223856
Closed Sun. (except in summer).
Elegant Venetian dining
(indoors and outdoors).
Moderate

caffè.

Trattoria alla Madonna
594 Calle alla Madonna
041/5223824
Rialto vaporetto
Near the Rialto, this *trattoria* specializes in grilled fresh fish. You will also find pasta and meat dishes on the menu and Venetian specialties like *fegato alla veneziana* (liver and onions).
Inexpensive-moderate

Al Vecio Canton
4738A Castello.
San Zaccaria vaporetto.
Located near Campo S. Provolo.
041/5285176
Closed Tue.
Family-run restaurant serving Venetian specialties and specializing in grilled meats.
Moderate

Vino Vino
2007A Ponte delle Veste.
S. M. del Giglio vaporetto.
Located near Campo S. Angelo and Campo S. Fantin.
041/5237027
Closed Tue.
Popular wine bar and restaurant serving typical Venetian cuisine.
Inexpensive-moderate

Gambero Rosso
7 Piazza Marconi
0187/812265
Closed Mon. and some winter months.
Ligurian specialties at this Cinque Terre restaurant located on a cliff with a view of the sea.
Moderate

Invitation for Comments:

We like to think that we have been as thorough as possible, but we welcome any and all comments, additions and corrections from our readers. You can reach us at:

What Kind of Food Am I?
8223 N. Gray Log Lane
Milwaukee, WI 53217-2863
USA
Fax: 1-414-228-4917
e-mail: EATnDRINK@aol.com
  www.eatndrink.com

About the Authors:
Michael Dillon, when not operating his graphic-design firm, is planning his next meal. Design and illustrations in this guide are the work of Mr. Dillon.

Andy Herbach, when not engaged in the practice of law, is planning his next trip.

Both authors love to eat and travel extensively. They reside in Milwaukee, Wisconsin.

Bwon Appetito!